We Are the Engineers!

Margaret Bennett

We Are the Engineers!
They Taught Us Skills for Life

Melville-Brodie Engineering Company, Kirkcaldy

Margaret Bennett
Hon. Fellow, University of St Andrews

GRACE NOTE PUBLICATIONS
OCHTERTYRE

We are the Engineers! They Taught Us Skills for Life:
First published in 2015
by Grace Note Publications C.I.C.
Grange of Locherlour,
Ochtertyre, PH7 4JS,
Scotland

www.gracenotepublications.co.uk
books@gracenotereading.co.uk

ISBN 978-1-907676-66-6

British Library Cataloguing-in-Publication Data
A catalogue record for this book is available from the British Library

The text of Ewan MacColl's song 'We are the Engineers' (pages 124–125) reproduced by kind permission of Ewan MacColl Ltd.

This book is part of an oral history project, 'The End of the Shift', which records the skills and experiences of former industrial workers in Fife and Perthshire.

Grace Notes Scotland is grateful to the following sponsors

heritage lottery fund LOTTERY FUNDED

The Gannochy Trust

Fife COUNCIL

Grace Notes Scotland Handing on Tradition

Dedicated with gratitude
to Melville-Brodie Engineering Company
whose apprenticeship training set us up for life,
and to all the engineers who were trained by Melville-Brodie.

In loving memory of my father,
civil engineer George Bennett (1917-2009),
who encouraged and inspired me.

CONTENTS

APPENDICES

PHOTOS & ILLUSTRATIONS

FOREWORD

Apprenticeships have been recognised for centuries as the foremost means of creating a highly-skilled workforce with practical prowess as well as theoretical knowledge. Through the apprenticeship system, craftsmen and women pass on their vast knowledge and expertise to a new generation. Kirkcaldy was at the centre of the skills revolution of the nineteenth and twentieth centuries.

Contrary to advice from tradesmen, business leaders and education experts, support for apprenticeships was diluted in the late 1980s and early 1990s, causing a vacuum in the country's skillbase.

Fortunately this is now being reversed, and we are beginning to see a return to the high standard of apprenticeships required to provide the skill levels needed by business to exploit the market opportunities available. Future training through apprenticeships will be a vital component of growth in skilled employment required to service a growing economy.

RT. Hon. Gordon Brown

Kirkcaldy, 2 June 2015

INTRODUCTION

Scotland's labour history has been the subject of many important studies, surveys, articles and books. Some of those published represent the invaluable collection of local groups and amateur historians, while others have been, and are, produced by academics and labour officials. The general expectation, even in Scotland, is that these works should be written in Standard English, regardless of the everyday speech of the workforce. For this publication, however, it seemed more important to transcribe, as recorded, the voices of folk whose vitality of language and expression gives a brighter reflection of their experiences during work and leisure.

This book has grown out of an oral history project, 'The End of the Shift', which aims to record the working practices and conditions of skilled workers in Scotland's past industries. Publicity about the project caught the interest of a group of retired engineers, who had all served apprenticeships with a prestigious Kirkcaldy firm, Melville-Brodie Engineering Company. Having lived through times when Scotland seemed blighted by industrial closures, the engineers could identify with 'the end of the shift' as they had experienced the effect of closing down Melville-Brodie Engineering Company. The entire workforce was dispersed, and with it, the skills, expertise and wisdom of generations. Kirkcaldy also lost a company that had been the pride of Scottish engineering.

Over the years, as the retired engineers reflected on the radical changes that have taken place since their 'second to none' training, they began to realise the importance of recording knowledge and skills for posterity. They also wanted to remember the firm that trained them, and so they planned a memorial to be erected on the site of Melville-Brodie Engineering works. It was to be designed and made by the men themselves, and in May 2014, the group had the satisfaction of seeing the plaque unveiled by Mrs June Shanks, daughter of the celebrated engineer, Robert Burt Brodie. Standing beside her were the two oldest Melville-Brodie 'boys' (aged 94 and 89), Bob Thomson and Willie Black, and the Secretary of the Melville-Brodie Retired Engineers' Club, Dougie Reid. Councillor for Kirkcaldy East, Kay Carrington, who supported the project, represented Fife Council as she addressed the audience and the media:

> This is a really exciting project because it shows our past history, how we made a difference, not just in Kirkcaldy, but in the wider world. Melville-Brodie engineers did everything that we're proud of in Scotland. We need to keep the story alive to enable us to take that forward to children and grandchildren in the future.

Editorial notes on the preparation of the book

Over several get-togethers the retired engineers have shared their memories and experiences, and allowed their conversations to be recorded with a digital microphone. These recordings have all been transcribed verbatim, not only capturing information about the firm, but also the wit and humour that emerges when folk get together. As far as we know, there are no recordings of owners of the company, Robert Burt Brodie or his son, Jock, but they grew up speaking the same language as the men who worked with them: Scots, in all its shades of colour that characterise the Fifer. Across a few miles, only the locals can tell the differences, coastal or inland, town or country, and those finer shades might not be represented here. Nevertheless, the pages that follow will not be written in Standard English but will attempt to echo the conversations from which they emerge.

A few spelling conventions may need explanation: Vowels attempt to replicate speech, such as 'dae' and 'noo' (rather then 'do' and 'now').

After much consideration, the word 'I' has been standardised because, listening to the recordings, it is sometimes rendered 'Ah' and other times 'I'. (The same speaker may interchange the form within a sentence, so it seemed simpler to retain 'I'.)

The apostrophe is only used for the possessive form (the man's cap), in verb constructions where needed (haven't, isn't, it's), and where a letter is actually missing. It will not be used, therefore, for English words ending in '–ing' because in Scots there is no letter missing. There's nothin missin, but here's twa mair examples:

> It's aw the same tae me. [English word is 'all' but in Scots there are no letters missing, and that is how it is pronounced.]
>
> We're tryin tae write this wee buik but the phone's aye ringin.

Though a transcription cannot truly represent the speakers, we hope that through these pages, the voices of the engineers can still be heard. Even a faint echo may convey the characters of the highly skilled professionals and craftspeople, who owe their expertise to an apprenticeship with Melville-Brodie Engineering Company. In sharing their memories, they remind the world of Scotland's remarkable industrial heritage.

Acknowledgements

It will already be apparent that this book could not have been written without the collaboration of a large number of people who have shared their expertise, ideas, a great deal of time, numerous visits, phonecalls, and letters, not to mention hospitality and laughter. For each of us it has been a rewarding experience, as we began with the goal of recording industrial history, (perhaps putting together a wee book), and soon found the process so engaging that we have all discovered a wealth of information and made friendships that will far outlast the project. For this, we are all most grateful.

Conserving the oral history of this specialised area of industry is part of a Grace Notes Scotland project, 'The End of the Shift', which records the experiences of workers in past industries of Perthshire and Fife. The wider project includes mines, mills, dye-works, bleachworks, and other factories, and is jointly funded by Heritage Lottery and the Gannochy Trust. On behalf of all who have taken part, Grace Notes Scotland accords sincere thanks to our sponsors for supporting a project that not only benefits a wide number of people but will also leave a lasting legacy to Scotland.

We owe a huge debt of gratitude to everyone who contributed: first and foremost to all the Melville-Brodie engineers, especially Dougie Reid, who got in touch with Grace Notes Scotland, coordinated numerous meetings, discussions, and visits, and inspired his former colleagues to take part. Their names are in the pages that follow, and on their behalf we would like to thank Dougie. He also contacted Fife Council, and we appreciate the efforts of Councilor Kay Carrington, whose enthusiasm helped secure funding for the Melville-Brodie Memorial Plaque, unveiled in Kirkcaldy on May 14, 2014. Dougie then contacted Mrs June Shanks, daughter of Robert Burt Brodie, who shared family photos and personal information with us, adding significantly to the project. We would all like to thank June for her contribution and for her generous hospitality.

From the outset, there has been a team of hard-working individuals who have sustained the project through every stage: Hazel Cameron, Jennifer Meiklejohn, and Talitha MacKenzie undertook the mammoth task of transcribing the audio-recordings; Chris Miles took part in the interviews and contributed her own memories; Gonzalo Mazzei scanned archive photos and family collections and also filmed and photographed throughout the project; Hugh Hoffman of the Fife Family History Society provided information from their archives; George Proudfoot of Kirkcaldy Civic Society sourced the only photo of Melville-Brodie Engineering Company, and Tom Harris in Kirkcaldy tracked down two Melville-Brodie photos from the early 1900s. We would like to thank the Scottish Archive of Print and Publishing History Records for permission to include an interview from 2002, particularly Dr Sarah Bromage (now at the University of Stirling), who made the recording, and Prof. David Finklestein at the University of Edinburgh, who led the project about Scotland's paper-making industry. Further thanks go to Fife Libraries and Archives as well as the National Library of Scotland in Edinburgh for helping trace written records, and to the newspaper editors who have granted permission to include excerpts.

Our gratitude and appreciation goes to Peggy Seeger, tireless activist and song-maker who, with her life-partner Ewan MacColl, made the world more aware of the lives of working people – together, and individually, they have raised voices in song, to remind (and sometimes shame) those in high places that workers deserve a decent standard of living. For this project, Peggy has not only given permission to include Ewan's song, 'We Are the Engineers' but has also advised on both text and context of their involvement with the Amalgamated Union of Engineering Workers. The Melville-Brodie engineers are proud to be members of their union and are overwhelmingly grateful for the interest and support that Peggy has shown.

Thanks are also due to the Rt. Hon. Gordon Brown, former MP for Kirkcaldy, who wrote the foreword to the book. When the manuscript was complete, Ros and Russell Salton patiently proof-read the text, saving the writer from the embarrassment of typographical and other errors that would have marred the publication. A huge 'thankyou' to Ros and Russell, and if any flaws have crept back in during a final edit, I take full responsibility and invite further amendments. For the layout, photographic production and typesetting we appreciate the expertise and support of Gonzalo Mazzei of Grace Note Publications C.I.C. (a Community Interest Company). And finally, though the names may not appear on the pages, we would like to acknowledge everyone who participated in any way, from offering small snippets of information to welcome cups of tea and hospitality. Our heartiest thanks goes to one and all.

Margaret Bennett
Hon. Fellow, University of St Andrews
'The End of the Shift' project leader
Grace Notes Scotland
Scottish Charity SC040434
'Dedicated to handing on traditions'

The project, start to finish.

p. 7

Photo 1: Planning the project, 21 August 2013

Photo 2: Dougie Reid (L) and John Greig (R) interviewed by Margaret Bennett

Photo 3: Willie Black interview

p. 8

Photo 4: Ronnie Fleming (L) and John Greig (R) discuss drawings

Photo 5: Left to Right: Margaret, Dougie, John, Ronnie and Willie, 2013

Photo 6: Collecting drawings, plans and photos, 19 February 2014

p. 9

Photo 7: Dougie explains drawings to Chris Miles, 19 February 2014

Photo 8 & 9: John and Dougie discussing historical information of Melville-Brodie Eng. Co with Margaret, 26 August 2014

1

2

3

4

5

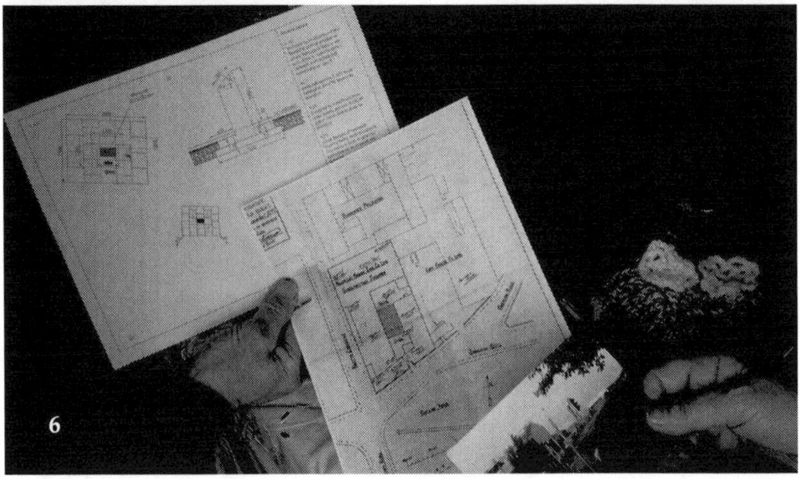

6

7

8

9

Almost ready to go to press: Margaret Bennett with Ronnie Fleming and Dougie Reid. Monday, 1st June 2015. [G. Mazzei].

PART 1

Kirkcaldy: A Cradle of Scottish Engineering

William Main Melville was born in 1846 in a town that was alive with industry, shipping and commerce – Kirkcaldy. Just a year earlier, when asked to describe his parish for the 1834-45 *Statistical Account of Scotland,* local minister, the Reverend John Alexander, reported that, 'A spirit of enterprise prevails'.

In the 19th century, the place was abuzz with trade and had an international reputation that might have rivalled any city in Europe. The earliest manufacturing skill had been nail-making, an ancient craft developed in medieval times on the outskirts of town. Kirkcaldy's most famous son, Adam Smith (1723-1790), described how he first contemplated his concept of 'division of labour' by watching the nail-makers at Pathhead. His work in preparation was the book that is said to have changed the world: *Inquiry into the Nature and Causes of Wealth of Nations* (1776).

Then, as now, skilled craftsmen were not made overnight, but spent years learning the tricks of their trade. Watching them work, Smith was struck by the meticulous attention to detail that turned boys into expert craftsmen:

> A common smith, who, though accustomed to handle [sic] the hammer, has never been used to make nails, if he is obliged to attempt it, will scarce be able to

> make above two or three hundred nails in a day, and those, too, very bad ones. The smith who has been accustomed to make nails, but whose sole or principal business has not been that of a nailer, can seldom, with his utmost diligence, make more than eight hundred or a thousand nails in a day. I have seen several boys, under twenty years of age, who had never exercised any other trade but that of making nails, and who could make upwards of two thousand three hundred nails in a day.
>
> The making of a nail, however, is by no means one of the simplest operations. The same person blows the bellows, stirs or mends the fire as there is occasion, heats the iron, and forges every part of the nail: in forging the head, too, he is obliged to change his tools. The different operations into which the making of a pin, or of a metal button, is subdivided, are all of them much more simple, and the dexterity of the person, of whose life it has been the sole business to perform them, is usually much greater. The rapidity with which some of the operations of those manufactures are performed, exceeds what the human hand could, by those who had never seen them, be supposed capable of acquiring.[1]

Adam Smith also noted that they relied on a wide team of people to source and supply the raw materials needed for nail-making. The journeyman craftsmen were a close-knit group, with their own guild, recognized as one of the ancient Scottish Guilds. Old gravestone inscriptions call them 'nailers', identifying them as blacksmiths with a very specific skill. Examples of their hand-forged, square nails can still be seen in old buildings, from castles to cottages all over Scotland, and estate account books record orders for thousands of them.

While Pathhead was the main location for nail-making, there were others along the Fife coast. According to the Rev. George

[1] Adam Smith, *Inquiry into the Nature and Causes of Wealth of Nations*, pp. 13 – 14.

Muirhead of Dysart, writer of the *Old Statistical Account*, in the 1790s there were 43 'nailers' in Pathhead, with output of six million nails, annually exceeding that of the adjacent communities.[2] Thanks to recent research by historian John G. Harrison (2013), we now know that as far back as the 1500s Dysart nailers supplied nails for Holyrood House: "In 1531 an unnamed smith in Dysart supplied 1160 plensher nails and 800 door nails for work at Holyrood. In 1537-9 Robert Sille in Dysart supplied 19,800 door nails, 16,400 plensher nails…[etc]." Remarkably, however, in the 1600s the nails were sold via a distributor, 'the Dysart nailwife'. She was a widow whose name appears as Alison Fermer 'nailwyfe' in the accounts of the Master of Works of Holyrood Palace, whose transactions included, "payment of £694-8s-2d for nails for Holyrood" in 1672.[3]

Today, thanks to Fife Council, visitors to the area can see where they worked, as one of locations has been preserved as a museum. Retired engineer John Greig, who grew up hearing the local traditions, was familiar with it:

> There's a cave[4] along the Fife Coast, not that far along from Kirkcaldy, Wemyss Cave – it's now a museum attraction. There's pockets on the wall o this cave and you can see where they worked. And caves like this one were what we'd now call 'industrial lets'. They were the premises used by the nail-makers.

The metal used by the nailers came from far and wide, as Dougie Reid, secretary of the Retired Engineers Club, explained:

> The nails were made from scrap iron, brought to them by folk from around the area, but when the demand

[2] *Statistical Account of Scotland 1791–1799*, Vol. 12, pp. 506–14.

[3] John G. Harrison, "Notes on the History of the Nail Trade in Scotland 1500–1800" (2013. Now available online via his website, <www.johnscothist.com>.)

[4] In his booklet, *Guide To Wemyss Caves*, local historian Frank Rankin describes "Johnathan's Cave", which was home to a nail-maker and his family in the 18th century. See pp. 29–33 and location map, p. 44. (Published by Save Wemyss Ancient Caves Society, Methil, Fife, 1988, revised and reprinted 2009.)

> outstripped the supply they had to import it from Europe. So there was a lot o trade between Kirkcaldy and ports of the Fife coast with ports in Denmark and more on the Flemish coast. And these ships brought over the scrap, so the iron could be used for nails. They were made on a small anvil, called an oliver, and they were usually square, flat-sided. They made all sort o different lengths, from wee tacks right up to big, muckle nails – not just for buildings, but the only means o transport then was horse power, an horses had to be shoed. And depending on the type o horse, the blacksmith makes the shoe and it has to be nailed on with different sizes of nail, and the supply was these square, tapered nails.

Describing the situation in the 1790s, the Rev. Muirhead noticed, however, that "some of the nail-makers are becoming weavers". Their trade was declining, as Dougie pointed out :

> When the Industrial Revolution was starting to take off, things changed. And it really took off big time in Scotland when the Carron Iron Works in Falkirk started to make wire, drawn wire. And they offered the wire to the nail-makers, but the Kirkcaldy craftsmen had a very, very strict Guild – they did all their own work, start to finish. Talk about closed shop an craft protection an all the rest o it! An of course they said "No, we want nothing to do wi that." So they completely shut off, from that market – they didn't want anything to do wi it. But, of course, you cannae stop progress, and eventually, the nails got cheaper an cheaper an cheaper, because the new method was easier – much easier with the wire. And so the nail trade went down and when it finally collapsed, the men had to get other work.
>
> Kirkcaldy's main industry was linen and it goes back a long time. In 1750 the planned village of

> Sinclairtown was specially laid out for linen workers – that's the area of Kirkcaldy where we worked, but few buildings of that era remain, so you can't really see it today. The name is still used – Sinclair was one of the two main landowners in Kirkcaldy. And the linen industry was based originally on locally grown flax, spun and finished by handloom weavers.[5] To begin with, it employed mostly women but gradually it included men who had become redundant with the collapse of the nail-making trade.
>
> Then, after the invention of the steam engine and the power loom, spinning and weaving factories appeared. One of the earliest was a canvas-weaving factory set up in 1848 by Michael Nairn, for making linen and canvas products. He had studied the making of floorcloth, so he set up his own factory and developed it from there, making linoleum. There were several other factories built at Victoria, Hawkleymuir, St. Clair, Parkhead and one in Denfield, which was later owned by the Main family. When they opened the Dunnikier Mine (The Pannie Pit, as we called it), there was plenty of coal to supply these factories. That pit was located at the site where the Fife Council now has the recycling depot and years ago these works covered both sides of Beattie Crescent – at that time it was called Factory Road.

As the Rev. Alexander noted in 1845, the "principal trade of the town is the manufacture of various descriptions of linen, with the collateral branches of flax-spinning, bleaching, and machine-making". In his description, he attributed the success of the Kirkcaldy linen industry to the engineers who designed and made the machinery and to those who maintained them:

---

[5] By the 1790s, Kirkcaldy linen makers were importing flax from Riga for their white cloth as well as from Dutch and German markets for other types of linen. OS, p. 514.

> The progress and prosperity of flax-spinning called for engineers and machine-makers, consequently, a large and important branch of this trade has recently sprung up. There are in this parish three works, engaged chiefly in making steam engines, and flax-spinning machines, in executing mill-wright work and in founding iron and brass. In these three works 200 men, at an average wage of 15s. per week, are employed. The mills in the district have not furnished sufficient employment for these [engineering] establishments... but extensive orders have been executed in them for Ireland, the continent of Europe, and the British colonies.[6]

Engineers had already begun to make their mark in Kirkcaldy by 1793 when the first flax-spinning machines were introduced. The town saw its first steam engine in 1807, fuelled by coal from the Pannie Pit, and soon industry was transformed by mechanization, as Dougie explained:

> Steam from a coal boiler to a steam engine must have driven the overhead shafting, which in turn, by belt drive, was the motor-power to the individual machines. There was no electricity until around 1890, and then only direct current, initially generated from a steam engine. In those days, Kirkcaldy was also the centre of the Scottish pottery industry – there were several potteries, including Fife Pottery that produced Wemyss Ware, they're famous for their Tabby Cat, worth a fortune today.[7]

At the mention of Fife Pottery, Kirkcaldy-born Chris Miles recalled that it was situated in Pottery Street, just across from

---

[6] *Statistical Account of Scotland 1834–45*, Vol. 9, Kirkcaldy, County of Fife, P. 756.

[7] A Wemyss Ware Tabby Cat could cost several thousand pounds and, judging by Sotheby's accounts from the 2004 Gleneagles auction, piglets are even more costly: two Wemyss Ware piglets fetched £70,000.

Gallatown School. After meeting some of the retired engineers in 2014 Chris remarked that their conversation brought back a long-forgotten memory from the early 1980s when she was Head Teacher there:

> The school is one of Kirkcaldy's lovely old stone buildings, which was built in 1862, and the second oldest school building in Fife still in use as a school. They added an extension in 1902, but you can hardly tell that it's been added on as it was so well done. But what comes into my mind at the mention of Wemyss pottery, is that one day, not long after I took over as head teacher, I arrived back from a meeting and there was an old man standing outside the school, just looking, looking at it, deep in thought. He'd have been in his eighties, and I asked if he was looking for someone, or wondered if I could help him. He said, "No, I was just standing here, remembering. I used to be a pupil at this school and it takes me back – I can just picture it like it was yesterday, over there, bouncing a ball in that corner. It hasnae really changed ..." So I asked if he'd like to come inside and look around, and he did. And inside the school was pretty much the same too. So I made him a cup of tea in my office and when we were sitting having the tea he told me that he remembered the day the Tsarina of Russia came with the Earl of Wemyss to the pottery. She was his guest at the time. And there they were, all the children lined up outside the school as they passed by, waving their flags – but he remembered they were mair interested in looking at the Earl's car than the folk in it, because there werenae many cars in those days! And he was telling me that the Tsarina had bought hampers and hampers of Wemyss crockery, just ordinary tableware from Gallatown Pottery, to take back as presents for her staff. The pottery wasn't making stuff they thought would turn out to

> be valuable in later years, they made ordinary dishes and ornaments for ordinary people. And then he remembered the man who became the most famous decorator of the pottery – he was a Czech, named Karel Nekola, and when his health deteriorated in 1910 the pottery had a little stone workshop built for him behind his house, across the road from the pottery, and the old man remembers seeing them deliver unfired pottery to this wee place so he'd paint them. Nowadays he's quite famous, but back then, he was just one of several decorators recruited from what was then Bohemia. But it's quite a thought, that this old man actually saw the Tsarina in Kirkcaldy, all those years before she was executed with the rest of the family during the Russian Revolution. And amazing as that seems, it's also pretty amazing that Kirkcaldy traded with countries all over the world.

The previous century, in the mid-1800s, the Rev. Alexander reported that the town had "established markets in Canada, the United States, South America, the West Indies and Australia as well as the continent of Europe and the British colonies" and trade was booming. There were 160 ships registered in Kirkcaldy that traded with North and South America, the Mediterranean, France, the Baltic, Cape of Good Hope and Norway. He had recently seen Kirkcaldy's two whaling vessels returning from South Georgia (1833) with 900 tons of whale oil, essential to the engineering works. As well as local shipping, "the foreign ships which usually trade to this port are Norwegian, Danish, Hanseatic[8], Hanoverian and Prussian," on average 92 vessels a year.

In the town there were fifteen schools, a Post Office delivering letters twice a day, five libraries, including a Mechanics' Library, and a Scientific Association, which held public lectures for all

[8] Northern Europe's ancient trading block, known as the Hanseatic League, began in northern Germany and took in ports around the Baltic Sea. It is now looked upon as the earliest form of a common market agreement.

who were interested. The Rev. Alexander expressed concern, however, that Kirkcaldy's fifty-four inns and ale-houses could have a detrimental effect on hard-working folk and their families.

The 'spirit of enterprise' turned Kirkcaldy into one of the liveliest engineering centres in the world. Apart from the Fleming Memorial Plaque in Kirkcaldy[9], however, Scotland has few reminders of the men themselves, despite the widespread evidence of their work – the iconic Forth Rail Bridge heads the list.[10] Considering the number of youngsters who learned and perfected their engineering skills in Kirkcaldy, it seems only right to remember them, for their expertise has benefited the much wider world.

Sandford Fleming was born and brought up just off the High Street and served his apprenticeship with John Sang Engineers and Surveyors. In 1845, when he completed his indentureship, he emigrated to Canada and settled in Ontario. Today, Canada has two engineering colleges named after him, and he is known across the nation as the man who made Canada's much-loved Beaver postage stamp. He had learned about pattern-making and moulding as a fourteen year-old apprentice in Kirkcaldy. These were only two of the skills perfected under the watchful eyes of journeymen tradesmen. He was particularly drawn to design, structure and construction, as Sang's firm was heavily involved with Kirkcaldy's harbour improvements and the development of the water system. It was the perfect hands-on work experience for apprentices who also attended night school to study mathematics, physics and aspects of engineering such as the properties of different woods and metals.

Still in his teens, Fleming completed his apprenticeship, collected his papers and, with his brother, headed for Canada, a fully qualified engineer. This is the 'boy' who introduced the construction of iron bridges, instead of wooden, to a country

---

[9] As the plaque is in Kirkcaldy's War Memorial Gardens, it may not immediately occur to visitors that it commemorates a civilian, Sanford Fleming, who was not a war veteran.

[10] Glasgow engineer William Arrol, who started his career as an apprentice blacksmith, oversaw the work from 1882 till its completion in 1890.

planning a coast-to-coast railway. At the age of 21, he also improved the design of ice-skates, creating the prototype of modern skates. He surveyed and mapped Toronto Harbour, and added to his credentials a myriad of achievements that would take another book. Fleming undoubtedly transformed Canadian engineering, yet he influenced a much wider world. And, true to his Kirkcaldy spirit of invention, while he was working on the railway, it occurred to him that trains needed to have a workable timetable, as daybreak is not at the same time in Vancouver as it is in Halifax. Thus it came about that he worked out and established Universal Standard Time.[11] Fleming introduced the system to Canada in 1879 and it was adopted universally in 1884.

Talented as he was, Fleming attributed his achievements and high standards of work to the firm who trained him: John Sang Limited. Who, then, were the Sangs? As Chris Miles (a well-known singer) commented, "When folk walk down Sang Road in Kirkcaldy, they don't really think about engineering, but some o us could imagine it has something ti dae wi singing!" Apart from his work on Kirkcaldy harbour, John Sang was the engineer responsible for sections of Kirkcaldy and Dysart Water, the construction of Harperleas Reservoir, and the conduit to Ballo Reservoir and Overton. He was also a member of the Kirkcaldy Naturalist Society for whom he wrote a paper, "The Structure of Wood", now a seminal work on the subject.

There are common threads that run through stories of engineering – some suggest it's all down to good teaching; others say it's in the blood. The Sang family may be a case in point as Kirkcaldy-born Edward Sang, a mathematical genius, invented the 'skew arch'. And, with the help of two of his daughters, Flora (1838-1925) and Jane (1834-1878), he also computed large tables of logarithms more advanced than the tables of European mathematicians. His arch was developed by his son, Edward Elmslie Sang, who went on to design bridges.

---

[11] To set up his idea of standard time, Fleming worked out divisions of 24 time zones, each an hour from the next and all a fixed number of hours from 0 degrees longitude – hence Greenwich mean time.

The world of Kirkcaldy engineers seemed to be a hotbed of creativity. There was a network of them, whose inspiration was to last for over a century and set standards of the highest calibre. As Dougie pointed out, there were very strong links between the different firms and industries: "But when you look at the wider picture, it wasn't just on a business level – these families all seemed to marry into one another. So there were generations of the same families that kept it all going." Among them was a youngster who was fascinated by the machines that operated his grandfather's power-loom factory, William Main Melville.

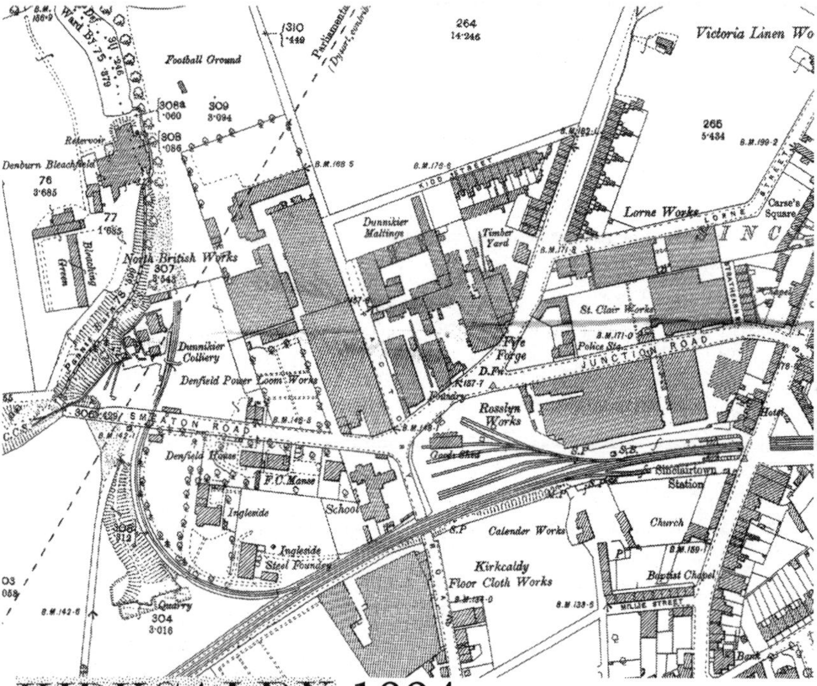

KIRKCALDY 1894

Map showing of the site of the Dunnikier Colliery (Pannie Pit), the Denfield Power Loom Works on Factory Road (now Beattie Crescent), and across the road (marked 'Foundry', opposite Fife Forge) is Melville & Henderson's, later to become Melville-Brodie Engineering Company.

[Ordinance Survey map, 1894]

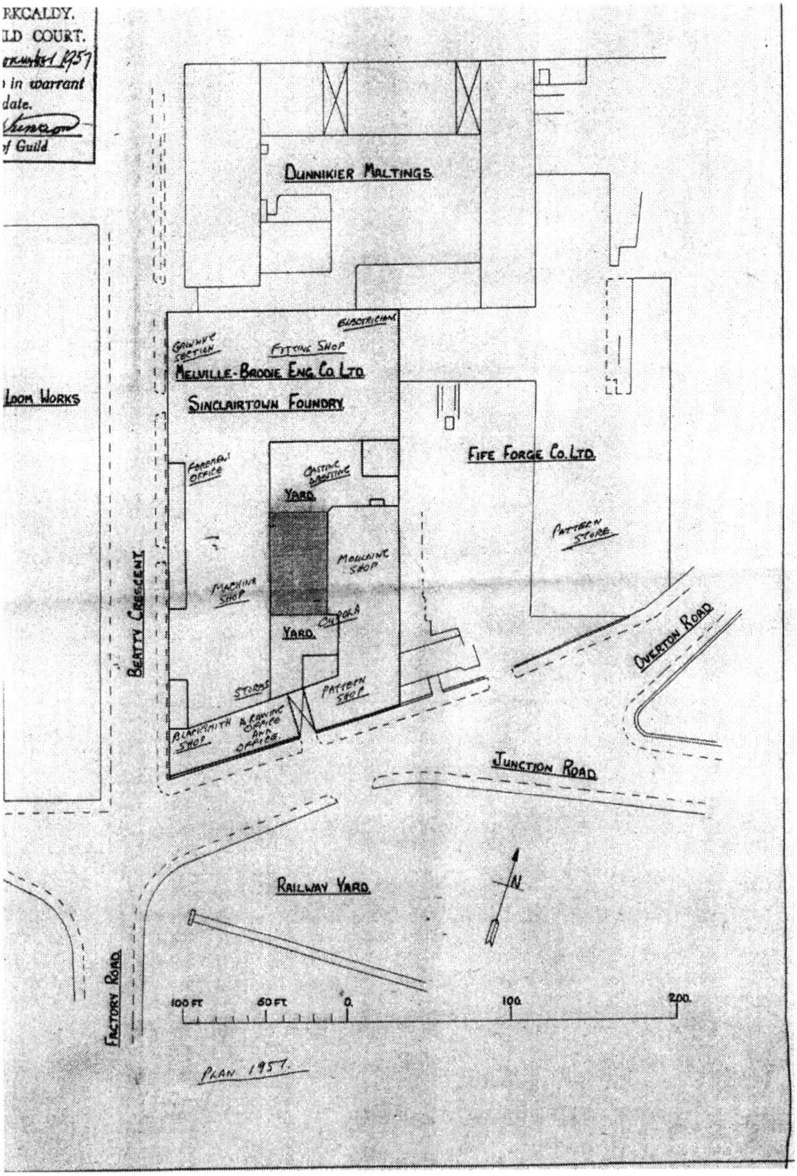

Drawing from a planning application, 1957, which shows the site of Melville-Brodie Engineering Company in relation to the Denfield Power Loom Works and Fife Forge.

[Fife Archive Collection]

William Main Melville

William Main Melville was born in 1846, the fifth and youngest child of John and Janet Melville (née Main). His father was a handloom weaver and his mother the daughter of John Main, who owned the Denfield Power Loom Factory.[12] The Melville family home was in Sinclairtown, close to what we now know as the 'business centre' of town. Sadly, however, John Melville died when William was only two. Being a close-knit family, the Mains were supportive of Janet and the children, and William grew up close to two cousins, John and William Main. The children seem to have had a lot in common and it is easy to imagine a grandfather taking a special interest in little boys with a passion for machinery.

While most children are mesmerized gazing at the magic of machinery, some want to know exactly how it all works. Watching the rows of spinning machines in their grandfather's factory, William and his cousins soon understood that if any machine broke down, the factory would grind to a halt. As William developed an early aptitude for engineering, mechanical work, problem-solving and innovating, he followed in the footsteps of previous generations when he became an apprentice engineer. Though there is no written evidence, it is likely that he began work at the Denfield Powerloom Factory and was still in his teens when he completed the meticulous training. By 1867 the number of factories in the town had increased to eighteen, operating 1,612 power looms.

In 1869, John Main gave his grandson a head-start in business by setting up work premises for him directly across the road from the Denfield Powerloom Factory. From this office, with a smiddy, a machine shop and fitting shop, they could service the Denfield

[12] According to records held by the Fife Family History Society, John Melville was a leather-merchant. Though Kirkcaldy's leather industry has long disappeared, during the hey-day of the horse it was the town's second most important trade. *The Old Statistical Account* for Kirkcaldy (1798) reports on the huge trade in imports of hides as well as bark used for tanning: see p. 39. When machines were introduced there was also a great demand for leather to make machine belts.

machinery. As Dougie suggested, however, John Main was close to retirement and saw an entrepreneurial opportunity to benefit both the factory and the young engineer. Consequently, William M. Melville went into business with local iron founder, Robert Henderson to establish a new company, Melville and Henderson, a complete engineering manufacturing complex.

On February 15, 1872, when he was twenty-five, William M. Melville married Euphemia Fraser and they had three daughters, Elizabeth, born in 1873, Janet in 1875 and Robina in 1877. The family lived at Smeaton Road, Sinclairtown but sadly, in 1887, when the girls were still young, their mother died of peritonitis at the age of forty-one.[13] Aside from genealogical records, little is known about the family life of William Melville and his daughters.

Kirkcaldy continued to earn a world-wide reputation in industry, and besides linoleum production, iron founding and engineering were crucially important. By the 1890s the firm employed over 80 people of varying skills, turning out superior types of machinery capable of improving the efficiency of factories and other machine-users. Their high standard of general engineering trades and foundry skills earned Melville and his firm a reputation for turning out the finest plant for any industry, at home or abroad. Local coal mines, textile mills, paper-makers and bottling plants relied upon them for essential equipment for these industries. As the local newspaper advertised, the firm offered "complete plants designed, supplied and installed" and a range of machinery that included steam engines, pumps, portable winders, elevators, paper rollers and other stationery machinery, rice and oil mill machinery, floorcloth and linoleum machinery.

To meet the demands of so many industries, the firm required engineers capable of understanding design, production and maintenance of an enormous range of machine. Melville and Henderson were well known in Kirkcaldy's business world, especially among owners of linoleum factories, textile mills, bottling plants, paper mills, and coal mines, for they relied on

[13] Thanks to Hugh Hoffman of the Fife Family History Society for searching the records and providing information on William Melville's family.

their firm for good engineers. As Dougie and several of his friends remarked, "It wasn't just for supplying and fitting, but especially for maintenance. A break-down in a machine is the last thing a factory needs."

From the day his training began, an apprentice engineer firmly understood that Melville and Henderson would not put their names to any indentureship papers unless the standards were met in every aspect of the job. At the end of the apprenticeship, when the 'boys' became time-served journeymen, they usually moved on to work with other firms. A few went abroad, some joined the Merchant Navy, and others found employment locally. Kirkcaldy's five linoleum factories, on the lookout for skilled engineers, also offered opportunities to gain specialised experience in that line of industry. There was a network within the workforce of local factories and mills, where skills were at a premium and managers kept an ear to the ground for talented engineers. In 1908, for example, one of Melville & Henderson's top engineers, Alexander Christie, was hired to be in charge of installing a wax extraction plant for Russell's Paper Mill. The new machinery was needed for the production of esparto paper (high quality paper used by artists and book binders), and the manager of Russell's Paper Mill was so impressed by Melville & Henderson's engineer that he later recruited Christie for the papermill. Once in a while, however, some might return to the firm, such as Robert Burt Brodie who had spent several years as a senior engineer with Barry, Ostlere and Shepherd. Though highly regarded in the linoleum factory, Brodie rejoined his old company when he was attracted to a job in the drawing office. Before long he was promoted to the design section as he had an aptitude in that area of engineering.

William Main Melville's business partnership lasted until 1908 when Robert Henderson retired and the company returned to the sole ownership of Melville. On June 30, 1908, the following notice appeared in *The Edinburgh Gazette*:[14]

[14] See p. 710.

NOTICE OF DISSOLUTION.

THE Firm of W. M. MELVILLE & HENDERSON, Engineers and Ironfounders, Sinclairtown Foundry, Kirkcaldy, has been DISSOLVED by mutual consent of the Subscribers, the sole Partners thereof. The Business will be carried on by the Subscriber William Main Melville on his own account and under the name of W. M. MELVILLE.

Mr. Melville is authorised to uplift all the debts due to, and he will discharge the whole debts and liabilities of, the Firm.

Dated this 24th day of June 1908.
W. M. MELVILLE.
Witnesses to the Signature of William Main Melville—
W. KILGOUR, Clerk, 31 Aitken Street, Kirkcaldy, Witness.
R. CARGILL, Clerk, 102 Dunnikier Road, Kirkcaldy, Witness.

ROBERT HENDERSON
Witnesses to the Signature of Robert Henderson—
AND. NICOLSON, Solicitor, Edinburgh, Witness.
J. MACKAY SMITH, Law-Clerk, 6 Duke Street, Edinburgh, Witness.

Apart from historical interest, the notice hints at the ethos that became the hallmark of every engineer associated with the firm: "Everything had to be done properly". In 1909, William Kilgour, whose signature appears above, was taken on as a 'sleeping partner' in the firm, and in 1910, he and Melville took on Robert Burt Brodie as a third partner. By this time, Melville was impressed by Brodie's management skills as well as by his professional talent, and, having reached the stage where he was planning to retire, Brodie's appointment gave Melville the assurance that he would be leaving the company in good hands.

Having started with the firm as a boy apprentice, Brodie lived up to Mr. Melville's expectations. The collaboration continued until 1918, when, at the age of 72, William M. Melville retired. *The Edinburgh Gazette* announced the retirement of Melville & Henderson's senior partner and informed the public that: "As of the 13th of October [1918] …The business will continue to be carried on by the Subscribers, Robert Burt Brodie and Wm Kilgour, under the name of The Melville Brodie Engineering Company."

From then on, the name of Robert Burt Brodie was to become embedded in the history of the firm. And, as far as this story is concerned, Brodie is also the link between the voices of twentieth century engineers and past accounts, which rely on archives, newspapers and written records. The history of the firm began to come alive when Dougie Reid was introduced to Brodie's youngest daughter, June, now in her eighties and living in Fife. Since her marriage over six decades ago, she is Mrs June Shanks, and she welcomed Dougie's enquiry. Over several visits, June shared her memories and photograph-albums with him and was also willing to be interviewed to help piece together the history of her father's firm. Though she was just six when Robert Burt Brodie died, June grew up hearing about him from the rest of the family as well as from a wide circle of friends and acquaintances: "He was very much a self-made man – he left school at twelve." The pages of notes jotted down during conversations, as well as scanned photographs, make an invaluable contribution to preserving the history of the Melville Brodie Engineering Company.[15]

[15] As June preferred not to be audio-recorded, the hand-written notes from an interview provide the information quoted here. In keeping with the rest of the book, it is presented in a conversational style, though should not be regarded as word for word quotation.

Robert Burt Brodie

Robert Burt Brodie was born in Dysart in 1869. He was given his middle name, Burt, as the family was connected to Burt the Stationerss in Kirkcaldy. His father worked as a warehouseman in the paper trade, and Robert attended the local school, just a few classes ahead of a little boy who eventually became Lord Tweedsmuir – John Buchan (b. 1875), author of *The 39 Steps*.[16] In those days the school leaving age was twelve[17], so in 1881 Robert began to serve his engineering apprenticeship with Melville & Henderson. Among June's photographs is one of the workforce from that time, showing just how young the apprentice boys were as they stood beside the men.[18] Scarcely sixteen when he completed his indentureship, Robert was keen to develop his inventive ability and so continued to study to a more advanced level. Since Kirkcaldy had a Mechanics' Library, the town was well placed to support night school students, who could also attend the public lectures at Kirkcaldy's Scientific Association. In 1888 Robert sat the Advanced Stage Examination in Machine Construction and Drawing validated by the Department of Science of Privy Council on Education, and was one of few students to be awarded First Class in the Advanced Stage certificate.[19]

In those days, Kirkcaldy was internationally famous for linoleum production and it was as easy to buy Kirkcaldy floorcloth in New York or Dunedin as it was in Glasgow or Edinburgh.[20]

[16] At the time, Buchan's father was Minister of Pathhead Free Church.

[17] After the passing of the Education Act of 1918, the school leaving age was raised to fourteen.

[18] In June Shanks collection, the back of the photo is labelled Dysart, so it is possible that the youngest and smallest boy may be Robert Burt Brodie.

[19] The exams were assessed by national standards and that year there were over 10,000 candidates in the UK. Just over 3 percent attained a First Class Advanced Stage certificate.

[20] Newspaper archives around the world carry advertisements as well as announcements of the firm's representatives. For example, *The New Zealand Evening Post* carried the following notice on March 10, 1906: "New Zealand representative for Barry, Ostlere, and Shepherd, of Kirkcaldy, Scotland leaves by the Paparoa on Thursday to make arrangements for his firm's representation at the forthcoming exhibition."

Linoleum was big business, and to a competitive firm, employing a creative, inventive engineer such as Robert Brodie was an enviable advantage in the world market. According to the register of patents, Robert Burt Brodie collaborated with fellow Kirkcaldy engineer, A. Alison, inventing (among other things) an improved machine for rolling linoleum as well as a more advanced and efficient design of ram pumps.[21]

Robert Burt Brodie in the drawing office, c. 1910.

Brodie gained an excellent reputation during his years as engineer with Barry, Ostlere and Shepherd, and his career was still in its ascendancy when he accepted the invitation to rejoin his old firm. By this time he had married Ann Allan from Dundee and the couple had three sons and a daughter: John, Jessie, Allan and Robert. The family lived on Loughborough Road in Kirkcaldy and enjoyed a much better standard of living than Robert Senior had known growing up in Dysart. Sadly the youngest son, Allan, died in 1926, while he was in his teens, though June had heard very little about what happened. Both John (Jock) and Robert took an interest in engineering, and in 1914, when war broke out, the eldest son, Jock, joined the Royal Flying Corps.

---

[21] Online register, see <patent.ipexl.com/assignee/robert_burt_brodie_1.html>

Throughout the Great War, the company continued production, with emphasis on essential services. Meanwhile, Robert Burt Brodie became increasingly involved in the welfare of the local community, and was elected to Kirkcaldy Council in 1915. His commitment to improving the standard of living for everyone is evidenced in the fact that he served on a number of Council Committees, including the Tramways & Electric Light Committee, the Gas Committee, the Harbour Committee, the Fire Brigade Committee and the Finance Committee. A man of the people, Brodie's aim was to make a difference to everyday life, and, as well as supporting better living conditions, he also contributed to, and took part in, various social events, including the Kirkcaldy Gala.

In 1918, Jock returned return home, thankful to have survived a terrible war that had devastated so many families in Kirkcaldy.[22] By this time he was twenty-four, and hoped to join his father's engineering firm, but, at his father's insistence, he first had to attain more advanced qualifications. From 1919 to 1921, Jock attended Herriot Watt College in Edinburgh, (the world's first Mechanics' Institute) where he studied engineering and returned with the required diploma. By the time Jock joined the company as an engineer, Mr. Kilgour had reached retiring age. When he stepped down from his directorship, Robert Burt Brodie became the sole owner of the Melville-Brodie Engineering Company. His decision to retain the name Melville was a tribute to the engineer who had set a standard to which others would aspire. Brodie undoubtedly had enormous respect for William M. Melville, who died at the age of 77, just two years later.[23]

That same year (1921), having been re-elected to the Kirkcaldy Council, Brodie was a busy man. By this time the family had moved out of Kirkcaldy to Falkland, where Millfield House had become the Brodie family residence. With the appearance

[22] Kirkcaldy writer David Potter has brought together a stark and heart-breaking account of the town's role in the Great War. See, *'Tis a Hundred Years Syne: Kirkcaldy in World War I,* (Kirkcaldy Civic Trust), 2013.

[23] According to his death certificate, he died of cancer on 28 Dec 1923 at Rowanhurst, Kirkcaldy.

of motor transport, there was no longer a need to rely on horse-drawn vehicles, and it became feasible to commute. Although Scotland was at the forefront of the developing car industry, Robert Burt Brodie's pride and joy was a Buick car. As June showed photos from the Thirties of her father standing in classic pose beside his classic car, and her brother Jock in like manner beside a later model, it seemed odd that Brodie, an ambassador of Scottish engineering, would choose an American car. June explained, however, that her father became interested in Buick cars because the Buicks were from Arbroath although they emigrated to America and settled in Detroit.[24]

Browsing through a century of photographs and memorabilia, June shed light on her father's full and busy life – family man, engineer, business-man, community councillor, a man of many parts. Both sons were engineers, and his daughter, Jessie, became a nurse. Robert Burt Brodie was only in his fifties, however, when, sadly, his wife died. Though their children were adults, and Jessie had moved to Oxfordshire, a mother's death is a great loss to any family. There are few photographs of the family during that time, though several of the Melville Brodie workforce. They show aspects of life among the men: rows of bicycles reflect both leisure and transport of the day; men posed beside a work site are reminders of some of the Melville Brodie contracts as well as the daily attire – overalls and working caps. The photographs tell little of the family but mainly reflect the life of a very busy engineer and community councillor.

One holiday after her mother died, Jessie brought home a friend who travelled from Oxfordshire with her, a fellow nurse called Nancy.[25] As June put it, "She was a year younger than Jock. Her full name was Nancy Mary Grieve and that was it – she and my

[24] David Buick was born Arbroath in 1854 and was very young when his family emigrated to America. At the age of fifteen, he began to train as a plumber then became an engineer as he had a great interest in steam-powered cars. He developed the design of the carburettor, patented his improvement, and founded the Buick Motor Company. Unfortunately his decision to go into partnership was a financial disaster from which he never recovered. Buick died in relative poverty in 1929.

[25] Nancy Mary Greive was born in 1895 and died in 1976.

father fell in love and were married. So he had a second family after the first had all left home." Looking at a photo of Millfield House, June points to the house in which she was born in 1931, home of her childhood and youth. She recalls the house being lit by gas lamps, oil lamps and candles and there was a household staff that included a cook, an upstairs maid and a downstairs maid. Neatly kept lawns and garden also suggest a maintenance staff, as the Brodies made full use of the house, extending hospitality to family and friends. Life was very different from what Robert Burt Brodie had known as a boy in Dysart: "He came from nothing!" June remarked, as she remembered that they used to dress for dinner every night, not merely when they had guests.

June was the third and youngest daughter of the marriage, and speaking of older sisters, Jen and Robin, she smiled as she described herself as 'the afterthought', for by that time her father was over sixty. Their mother talked little of her background in the south of England, and in those days, "children were not encouraged to ask such questions". As June's half-brother Jock was 38 when she was born, she only knew him are as a busy, working man. One particularly bright memory of her father, however, is his arrival home from work each day: he always wore boots with criss-cross laces, and when he sat in his chair, June would sit by him and undo the laces to remove his boots. It is only in adulthood, however, that anyone can appreciate just how special that moment can be – the end of a long day's work, when at last it's time to put your feet up. A five-year old, meanwhile, is just pleased to see her Daddy arrive home and has no need to know anything about an engineering company.

On October 26, 1937, local newspaper *The Dundee Courier* reported news of the previous day: "Death of Falkland Councillor, Head of Kirkcaldy Engineering Firm Mr. Robert Burt Brodie..." He was 68 years old, and June was only six and too young to appreciate the mark of respect paid to her father at his funeral on October 27. The following day it was reported in *The Courier:*

> Over 150 employees of Melville Brodie Engineering Company, Kirkcaldy, paid an impressive tribute

> yesterday to the memory of Mr. Robert Burt Brodie, Principal of the firm, who died at Falkland on Monday [Oct. 25]. In their working clothes, they joined the funeral cortege at Kirkcaldy Cemetery. The cortege was also met by a large number of local business men… [26]

Brodie's son Jock, who was in his early forties, took over the company as he had more than twenty years of experience working with his father. As the new company director, Jock was equally determined to maintain the high standards set by Melville Brodie Engineering Company.

As every year passes, there are fewer and fewer folk to remember what it was like to work for the company in Jock Brodie's time. Today, (2015), only those in their seventies and eighties might be able to share memories of the actual work or skills involved. But only folk in their nineties could possibly remember Robert Burt Brodie or recall what it was like in his day. After he retired, a recognition that "all this could disappear, and it's Scotland's heritage" motivated Dougie Reid to form The Retired Melville Brodie Engineers' Club. The group has been meeting in Kirkcaldy for seven years, but today there is only one retiree left, Bob Thomson, who remembers Robert Burt Brodie's time, for the others have all passed away. Though Mr. Brodie had just retired when Bob began, his presence was still felt among the workforce.

Last May (2014), at a gathering at the KUSI Club in Kirkcaldy, we asked 94 year-old Bob if he remembered those days. His face lit up as he began:

> This is the sort o thing that, when you sit on a chair noo an something goes through your heid, like the time at Melville Brodie's, an you might laugh, for it brings back memories. Well often, I'm sayin tae my

[26] As June pointed out, the report in *The Courier* is not entirely accurate because her father was not (as stated) one time manager of Nairn's factory, as he had been the engineer at Barry, Ostlere and Shepherd.

family when they come tae visit, an I've been sitting here thinkin aboot things, I says, "I better tell them that." An then I says tae them, "I better tell ye that in case I dinna get the chance tae tell ye again."

An original badge fitted on the bearing cover of paper-making machines, showing the maker's name.

Journeymen and apprentices, Dysart, in the early 1880s, when five-year apprenticeship began at the age of twelve. (On the reverse side of the photo is: Robert Burt Brodie 1869–1937, No. 64 Dysart).

[June Shanks collection]

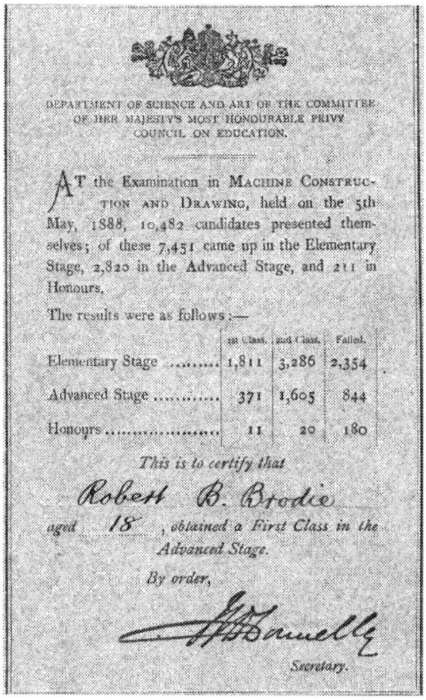

DEPARTMENT OF SCIENCE AND ART OF THE COMMITTEE OF HER MAJESTY'S MOST HONOURABLE PRIVY COUNCIL ON EDUCATION.

AT the Examination in MACHINE CONSTRUCTION AND DRAWING, held on the 5th May, 1888, 10,482 candidates presented themselves; of these 7,451 came up in the Elementary Stage, 2,820 in the Advanced Stage, and 211 in Honours.

The results were as follows:—

	1st Class.	2nd Class.	Failed.
Elementary Stage	1,811	3,286	2,354
Advanced Stage	371	1,605	844
Honours	11	20	180

This is to certify that

Robert B. Brodie

aged 18 *, obtained a First Class in the Advanced Stage.*

By order,

Secretary.

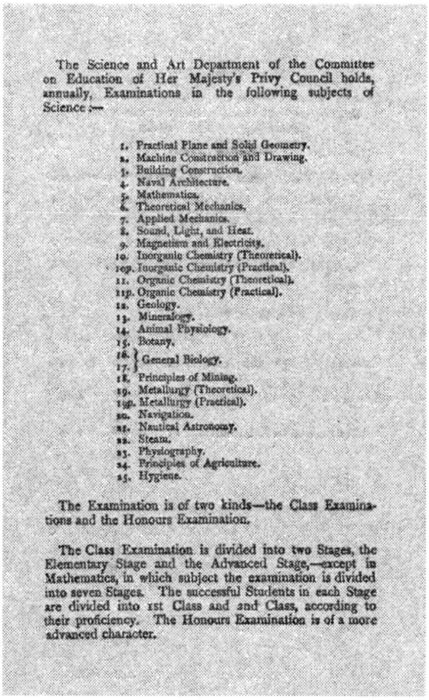

The Science and Art Department of the Committee on Education of Her Majesty's Privy Council holds, annually, Examinations in the following subjects of Science:—

1. Practical Plane and Solid Geometry.
2. Machine Construction and Drawing.
3. Building Construction.
4. Naval Architecture.
5. Mathematics.
6. Theoretical Mechanics.
7. Applied Mechanics.
8. Sound, Light, and Heat.
9. Magnetism and Electricity.
10. Inorganic Chemistry (Theoretical).
10p. Inorganic Chemistry (Practical).
11. Organic Chemistry (Theoretical).
11p. Organic Chemistry (Practical).
12. Geology.
13. Mineralogy.
14. Animal Physiology.
15. Botany.
16. } General Biology.
17. }
18. Principles of Mining.
19. Metallurgy (Theoretical).
19p. Metallurgy (Practical).
20. Navigation.
21. Nautical Astronomy.
22. Steam.
23. Physiography.
24. Principles of Agriculture.
25. Hygiene.

The Examination is of two kinds—the Class Examinations and the Honours Examination.

The Class Examination is divided into two Stages, the Elementary Stage and the Advanced Stage,—except in Mathematics, in which subject the examination is divided into seven Stages. The successful Students in each Stage are divided into 1st Class and 2nd Class, according to their proficiency. The Honours Examination is of a more advanced character.

Robert Burt Brodie's advanced certificate in Machine Construction and Drawing, 1888.

Junction Road from St. Clair Street, 1908. At the top of the street, in the distance, is Melville-Brodie Engineering Company. [George Proudfoot, Kirkcaldy Civic Society; in *Bygone Kirkcaldy* Eric Eunson, Stenlake Publishing 1991].

Robert Burt Brodie

Melville-Brodie workforce, c. 1934.

Melville-Brodie engineers, makers and fitters of the machinery for Tayside Lino Factory, Newburgh, Fife, 1912.

[June Shanks collection]

Falkland Lino Factory (derelict in 2014). It was officially opened in 1934, when Robert Burt Brodie was among the guests' as Melville-Brodie made and fitted the machinery.

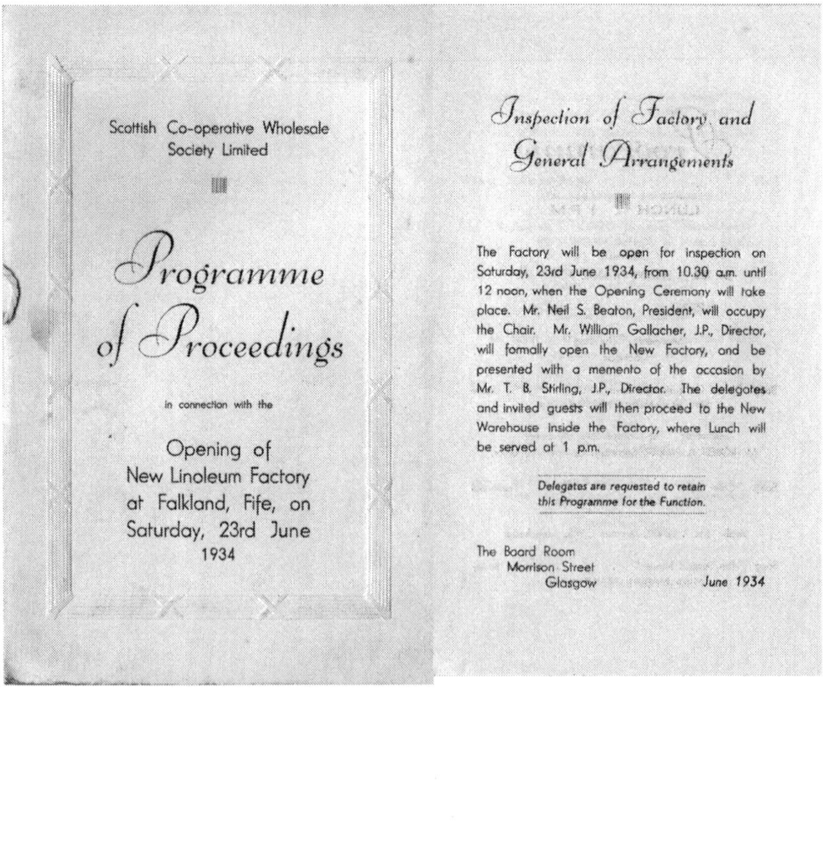

Scottish Co-operative Wholesale Society Limited

Programme of Proceedings

in connection with the

Opening of New Linoleum Factory at Falkland, Fife, on Saturday, 23rd June 1934

Inspection of Factory and General Arrangements

The Factory will be open for inspection on Saturday, 23rd June 1934, from 10.30 a.m. until 12 noon, when the Opening Ceremony will take place. Mr. Neil S. Beaton, President, will occupy the Chair. Mr. William Gallacher, J.P., Director, will formally open the New Factory, and be presented with a memento of the occasion by Mr. T. B. Stirling, J.P., Director. The delegates and invited guests will then proceed to the New Warehouse inside the Factory, where Lunch will be served at 1 p.m.

Delegates are requested to retain this Programme for the Function.

The Board Room
Morrison Street
Glasgow

June 1934

Programme

LUNCH .. 1 P.M.

Chairman:
Mr. NEIL S. BEATON, President, S.C.W.S. Ltd.

BLESSING LUNCH

Sentiment: "The King"
Chairman

Song "In an Old-fashioned Town" . . . Squire
MR. ALEXANDER MACGREGOR

Sentiment: "The Co-operative Movement"
Mr. ROBERT A. PALMER, Secretary, Co-operative Union

Song "Caller Herrin'" . . . Traditional
MISS ANNE BALLANTINE

Reply: Mr. J. PENNY, Director, C.W.S., Manchester

Song "The Second Minuet" . . . Maurice Besley
MISS MARION MACGREGOR

Sentiment: "The Scottish Co-operative Wholesale Society and Success to the New Linoleum Factory"
Mr. JOHN CASSIDY, General Manager, Kinning Park Co-operative Society

Song "Maggie Louder" . . . . . Scots
MR. ALEXANDER MACGREGOR

Reply. Mr. T. HOPKINS, Manager, Linoleum Factory
Mr. DUNCAN CAMERON, J.P. Director, S.C.W.S.

Aria "Softly Awakes My Heart" . . . Saint-Saens
MISS ANNE BALLANTINE

Sentiment: "The Chairman"
Mr. JOHN M. BIGGAR, Chairman, Glasgow and District Co-operative Conference Association

Song "Deirdre's Farewell" . . . . Kennedy-Fraser
MISS MARION MACGREGOR

Reply

VOTES OF THANKS

Duet "Ye Banks and Braes" . . . . Burns
MISS MACGREGOR AND MR. MACGREGOR

"Auld Lang Syne"

PIANIST . . MISS BETTY GOVAN

Programme of Music by the S.C.W.S. Prize Band

1. Overture—"The Bohemian Girl" . . . Balfe
2. Selection—"The Maid of the Mountains" Fraser-Simson
3. Selection—"The Mikado" . . . Sullivan
4. Selection—"A Day wi' Burns" . . . arr. Hume
5. Selection—"The Desert Song" . . . Romberg
6. National Fantasy—"Scottish Minstrelsy" arr. Hawkins

Musical Director - Mr. GEORGE HAWKINS

Celebration for the coronation of King George V, Kirkcaldy, 11 May, 1911.

Presentation of the Freedom of the Burgh
to
Field Marshal, Earl Haig.
The Provost, Magistrates and Councillors of the
Royal Burgh of Kirkcaldy,
request the pleasure of Your Company
at the Cake and Wine Banquet in the
Beveridge Hall, Kirkcaldy, on Saturday,
10th July 1920, at 4.15 P.M.

R.S.V.P. to Town Clerk.

Councillor Robert Burt Brodie's invitation to a Civic Reception in Kirkcaldy for Field Marshall Earl Haig, 1920.

Staff outing, Robert Burt Brodie, standing at centre, 1909.

Melville-Brodie foremen's outing in front of the Lomond Hotel, Kinnesswood.
Pipe smoking gentleman back row, 1st left, is John Bayne, c. 1913.

John (Jock) Brodie, Royal Flying Corps, c. 1914.

Robert Burt Brodie in the garden of Milfield House, 1930s.

Robert Burt Brodie, standing by his Buick, c. 1929.

John (Jock) Brodie, same pose, different Buick, 1930s.

Milfield House, Falkland, Robert B. Brodie's family home from the late 1920.
[June Shanks collection]

Robert B. Brodie (1st left) and Melville-Brodie staff, 1920s. Over the years, most folk cycled to work.

[June Shanks collection]

PART 2

Apprenticeships in the Thirties and Forties

Bob Thomson was born near Markinch, in Coaltown of Balgonie, on June 14, 1920. In his day, the school leaving age was fourteen and, like most school-leavers, the main thing was to get a job as soon as possible. Every family expected it, and every youngster was given the responsibility to look for work. Looking back to a time when he was called 'Wee Bob', he remembered when he first tried to get a job he found it was far from easy:

I should have left school at fourteen but I couldnae get a job so I was sent back to school. My Dad says, "Back to school! You're no hingin aboot here daein nothin." So I went back to school an every Saturday, I'd go oot askin, could they gie me a job, a boy, as an apprentice, I was just askin for work. Eventually, after I'd been back at school for two terms, an still lookin for a job, I got word to go an see Mr. Williamson at Melville-Brodie's, an I got started as a turner! I was fourteen an a half when I started my apprenticeship in January 1935.

The manager of the company was Jock Brodie, having taken over from his father the previous year. Becoming an 'indentured apprentice' was a serious matter, as it would be the first time in a boy's life he would enter into a legally binding contract. The wording was as antiquated as the centuries-old system, binding an apprentice to his master. Granted, it had been proven to train the finest craftsmen in the world, but, to the uninitiated, the terminology has a fearful ring about it, reminiscent of servile conditions of indentured servants of earlier times.

The front cover, printed with the name of the company, bears Bob's name, ROBERT THOMSON, his age (14) and the name of his guardian (his father). The first clause states the names of those in agreement as well as the apprentice's address. A further twelve clauses spell out the terms under which Bob had agreed to serve. The second one, titled BINDING, illustrates the tone of the entire document:

> The Apprentice of his own free will, with consent of the Guardian, hereby puts and binds himself as a Trade Apprentice with, and to, the Employers in the *Turning* Department of their business subject to the provisions herein for the full and complete space of five years. The Apprentice and the Guardian bind themselves jointly and severally, that during the continuance of this indenture the Apprentice shall industriously and faithfully serve the Employers and promptly obey all the lawful rules, regulations, and commands of the Employers, and of their officers, representatives and authorised employees, and shall conceal and in no way reveal the secrets of the Employers' business or of the business of their customers, and also that the Apprentice will not do or commit, or suffer to be done or committed, any waste, damage or other injury to the property or goods of the Employers, and will not lend such property to any person without the consent of the Employers.

Although a fourteen-year-old might not understand every phrase of his indenture papers, there was no doubt in Bob's mind about the gravity of the commitment:

> I'll never forget my first day. I started on the Monday, an I was given aw the wee jobs, runnin aboot an that. An on the Thursday this man says to me, "Go away to the store an get me so-and-so." So I run, 14 year old, I ran doon intae the shop. You had to go doon three steps, an there was a door, which I pulled. There was a weight on that door that closed it, an when I closed it, who did I run into but Mr. Brodie? Right intae him! I was terrified, so I ran, an there was another door that took me oot tae the yard, so I ran oot there, an got back intae the shop the other way. But some o the men, or maybe the apprentices, saw what had happened, an said, "You'll be sacked. You'll get the sack!"
>
> Oh my God! Waitin aw that time tae get a job, an then going tae be sacked the first week!
>
> Anyway, as I was to find oot, what Mr. Brodie had done was, he went intae the stores, an got the storekeeper to find oot who I was. An then when they found oot who I was, the storekeeper was tae tell me that Mr. Brodie saw that I was in a hurry, but I didnae have tae run!

For the apprentice there was a lot to learn in five years, so from day one he had to pay close attention if he hoped to understand how the entire plant operated and how every step of each operation fitted together to complete production. There was a new vocabulary to take in, as every stage had technical terms that were part of general conversation among all the men. Learning who's who was essential, and eighty years later Bob laughed as he recounted how he first met the foreman of the blacksmith shop:

> You'd get sent for things, you see, an we had various things on drawins an that, an you'd come across various technical names. They'd say to you, "Go doon tae the blacksmith's shop an see Mr. Dunsire." He was the foreman, an I was told, "Ask him if he'll

> give you the long stand that we gied him last week."
> So you went away doon an asked him for this long stand. So you were left standin there!

Realising that he'd been the butt of a joke may not have seemed so funny at the time, but Bob soon realised that the apprentice had to learn how to deal with pranksters. They were everywhere, for the foremen themselves had been through it, and looked on such pranks as 'all in good fun' – it was a way of making sure the apprentice was paying attention, and that he wouldn't take offence. It was also part of toughening him up for the world of precision engineering, and, if Bob's remarkable recall is anything to go by, perhaps helped sharpen the wits and train the memory:

> Mr. Dunsire was the foreman in the blacksmith's shop. I could tell you aw the foramen's names. Bob Williamson was the foundry foreman, an George Inglis was pattern shop foreman, an, as I said, William Dunsire was the blacksmith. There was a shop manager caw'd Jim Bayne at that time, an the foreman of the machine shop was Willie Williamson. The fittin shop foreman was John Oliver. A lot were fae Kirkcaldy but Willie Williamson was fae Freuchie. There was another, a sort of charge-hand wi the apprentices up in the gallery. His name was Charles Ralley.

In Bob's day, the apprentices were given the task of setting and lighting the fires that provided the only heating in the work-spaces. It may have little to do with engineering, but the boys soon learned that even the most menial task, going for milk or chopping sticks for kindling, had to be done. Taking instructions was all part of the training (it says so in the indentureship agreement). But if the boys expected some grateful or even positive response, they could be in for an occasional surprise. Bob laughed recalling the daily fire-lighting duties:

> Every mornin when you got in at seven the apprentices kindled the fire – it was in a wee corner. Then when the first one was lit, they'd go on to the next one, an by the time you got them aw done, the first one was warmin up. An so you went up to the fire to get a heat, an they'd say to you, "C'mon, this is men's talk, get away fae here!" [laughter] An they'd chase ye away! That was all part o the apprentice system, it kept you in your place! Aye, you knew yer peckin order!

Finishing the apprenticeship and becoming a time-served journeyman was a real milestone in life. School leavers began as boys and, if they stayed the course, they finished as highly skilled young men, ready to take on responsibility.

Though Willie Black turned ninety in December 2014, he was 'just a boy' when he first met Bob, a time-served turner. Their friendship has endured over seventy years, and, not surprisingly, Willie shares Bob's sense of humour as well as bright, clear memories of his early days:

> I was born an brought up in Dysart – officially I'm William Black, an my date of birth is 17:12:24. I was about 15 when I left school, because bein born in December, I was caught at school so I didnae leave till the next year. That meant I was fifteen an a bit when I started my apprenticeship at Melville-Brodie's. It was my grandfaither who got me a job there – he didnae work there himsel, but he used tae work in an engineerin shop on the other side o the road, the Fife Forge Engineering Company[1]. My grandfaither an my uncle were at the same trade, an they worked at this heavy machinery. They used tae dae aw the shaftin work, everythin for ships[2] – an he heard there

[1] Fife Forge, founded in 1873 by the Harley family, made fittings for ships. At one time 150 people were employed, but by 1986 the number had been reduced to 30. (Recorded by BBC schools' project, The Doomsday Book.)

[2] See, 'Fife Forge', *The Glasgow Herald*, Nov. 9, 1967.

> was an openin at Melville-Brodie. Though we stayed in Dysart, an they stayed in Kirkcaldy, I was close to my grandparents because my mother used to take me doon once a week tae visit. My grandfaither an aw the family stayed away along near Starks Park, the football ground.

Though Dysart became part of Kirkcaldy in 1930, that mattered little to Willie who had a two-mile walk to work:

> I mind my first day. An Bob was there – he had been there afore the war started. An I mind you went in there like a wee laddie, an the foreman, he got hold of you, an he put you wi a tradesman an you had to start wi him. You weren't doing anything, you were just watchin, paying attention, an maybe you were there a week. Then you moved around after that week, an it spread on fae that.

Bringing home his first pay-packet was a proud moment for every apprentice and Willie recalls the exact amount:

> It was 9 shillings an 8 pence[3] an in those days you gied it to Mum. Oh, you were quite proud o your first pay packet! That was a help wi the hoose, an it made a difference to your Mum. Then she gied you somethin back, for your spendin money.

At home, as at work, the transition from boyhood to manhood began with the apprentice's contribution to household expenses. In Bob's day, the starting rate was 7/6 a week and it would be another four years before he saw a pound note in his pay-packet. According to the terms of his indentureship, a fifth-year apprentice would receive 20/- (shillings) a week, but, no matter the wage, the boys all knew that "You had to earn your keep."

---

[3] In today's currency, it was less than 50 pence (47 pence).

There was strict discipline at work and new apprentices soon learned that there would be no time-wasting, no idle chat, and sometimes no talking at all – at least not when the boss was around:

> Mr.Brodie was in charge o the machine shop at that time. It was his business, Robert Brodie's son, Jock Brodie, an we worked for him.... He would just walk up the middle o the machine shop, glarin, an back doon again. There would be no speakin to you, or you, or you!

Every day brought new experiences and challenges and on three evening a week, there was also night school. Despite the long days (7 a.m. to 4.30 p.m.), the apprentices took it all in their stride, and, as anyone who worked with him knows, Willie developed exceptional skills as a turner:

> Well it was lathes we used, an it depended on what job you were on whether you worked on metal, such as cast iron or brass. An I've seen us daein wood, for wooden rollers. As you know, a lathe is usually on the parallel, well, we used tae have vertical ones, because you made the tools tae suit whatever was required.
>
> Have you seen a paper mill, the big drying cylinders? Well, we used tae machine thae cylinders – surface grindin, cylindrical grindin, you had tae know aw that. But before that, durin the war, we were makin parts for aircraft carriers.

To become a precision engineer, "all that" includes knowing about the strengths and other features of different metals and woods as well as of the functions of tools and turning machines. Though the basic machine is the lathe, there are shapers, planers, and machines for drilling, milling and grinding. He has to learn to read and understand drawings and follow them exactly. He has to have excellent hand-eye coordination, an ability to calculate cutting speeds, and an awareness of health and safety issues. "We're no talkin stupid stuff, here!" He needs to have exceptional concentration, good balance and stamina, as he will often stand for long periods of time, continually adjusting the lathe's cutting edge. No matter the size of the job, a giant turbine or a tiny screw, the turner had to learn to work to a thousandth of an inch. In today's world of computers that set the machinery, such demands of accuracy seems like an impossible challenge. In Willie's day, however, it was all part of the job. Finally, if you were to stay the course and complete the apprenticeship, you needed a sense of humour:

> Oh, the place was full o pranks! They used tae tell you tae go for a long stand! [laughter] An you would go, an when you got there an asked, somebody would say, "Yes, hold on there," an you would maybe stand for quarter o an hour, half an hour, you'd still be there! Oh, but everyone just had tae take it. That was aw a part of the learnin, though you got wise tae it after a while – these boys will tell you the pranks that used tae go on!

As time went by, there were gradual pay rises: "It depended on the unions in those days, whatever rise the unions used to get you," and at the end of Willie's five-years he was earning over £2 a week, fully qualified at the age of twenty:

> You got your apprenticeship papers and, oh, everybody went oot tae celebrate. But in those days you couldnae get a drink until you were 21, or supposed tae be. So you couldnae go tae a pub at twenty – or not if folk knew you! Where I stayed in Dysart, everyone knew each other, an you couldnae go oot intae any o the locals because they knew you, or they knew your faither. So you just had tae go intae Kirkcaldy, an if no one knew you, you were lucky.

Though it was fairly common to have to look elsewhere for a job at the end of an apprenticeship, not surprisingly, Willie was kept on at Melville-Brodie's. There were standards to be kept up, there were new apprentices to be trained, and the manager expected the best.

Having worked at Melville-Brodie's through the Second World War, both Willie and Bob had experienced a side of engineering that neither of them had anticipated. They also lived through a time when every family in the country was affected, few areas more severely than in Fife.

The Wartime Years, 1939–1945

At the outbreak of war, conscription papers were sent to men aged between 18 and 41, though by 1942 the upper age had increased to 51 and the call-up included women aged 20 to 30. Only those whose work was regarded as essential or of national importance could be exempted. As decisions were made according to the National Service (Armed Forces) Act of 1939, all had to report, ready to serve. Among the young, there was a sense that a stint in the army would add adventure to life, with a chance to see more of the world. And so it was that the Melville-Brodie boys reported for duty.

Both men, engineer and apprentice, remember the call-up as well as the impact of war on the community, as Bob explained:

> My time was oot in the January then war started, September 1939. The reserved age at that time was 18 but the thing that happened fae then, when they were decidin who would go, the machine I was workin on, it was caw'd a capstan – it was a combination, an it was regarded as essential occupation. An so I never got intae the Forces. Probably just as well, but I mean, I wanted tae go! Oh aye, everybody was goin! So I ended up in the Home Guard – a lot of the apprentices were there. But now I think o the ones that never came back. There's a picture there an there's a chap facing us, he was a Pole, a friend o mine. His name was Lorenz Sobieski. His father was a Bank manager. I'm not sure whereaboot, but in this area, an he obviously was well-off compared tae me. He worked at Melville-Brodie's, an he was very friendly wi me. And, as a hobby, he went glidin, an he says, "You'll have tae come tae the glidin." So I says, "How much is it?" an he says, "Five pounds."
>
> Five pounds! An my wage only 7s 6d a week![4] Anyway, after the war started, when it come tae the

[4] Currently, £0.375 a week – less than 50 pence.

> bit you'd tae join up a lot o the boys would be in the Territorial Army, but Lorenz joined the RAF because of course he was able tae glide. An he was ta'en awa, an he lasted two weeks. He was dead in two weeks.
>
> An I remember there were three pals who worked wi us – two o them were brothers, their name was Pattison – Hugh, an I cannae remember the brother's name, an Roy Stewart the other boy – he served his time at Melville-Brodie's, an his time was oot before the war came along, an he had joined the Merchant Navy, because they need engineers. An on the Sunday mornin when war was declared he was on a ship comin back fae South America. An as it came through the Atlantic, war was declared at 11 o' clock, an at 12 o'clock his ship was torpedoed an he was away. Now his mother never believed till the day she died that he was dead. She wouldn't have it. An just up that street where they put the memorial up is where Roy Stewart used tae live.

The Pattison family was also to experience the awful heartache of loss as Hugh also joined the Merchant Navy and served on HMS Rawalpindi:

> Well Ludovic Kennedy's father was the Captain of the ship, an Hugh Pattison's brother served on it – it was an armed Merchant man. It had one gun on it an it was a member of the convoy, an they were attacked by a German ship. The convoy got away but they turned the gun on them, an they tried tae fight back. An that was him away too. Oh aye, an they were aw wi Melville-Brodie. You'll maybe remember there was a programme on television about Ludovic Kennedy, an he was talking about it.[5]

[5] Ludovic Kennedy was born in 1919 in Edinburgh. His father (b. 1879) was a Royal Navy officer, Captain Edward Coverley Kennedy, and in 1939 he was called out of retirement to captain HMS Rawalpindi. He was killed on 23 November 1939 when the ship was sunk north of the Faroe Islands, near Iceland.

Despite the tragic losses, there was no lack of willing recruits, among them, the apprentices who, like Willie, had just turned eighteen:

> We aw got a card, an twice Wull Lindsay an I went tae sign up, but the chap at the recruiting centre said, "Get tae –!" He says, "If I was startin you, takin you oot o a reserved occupation, I would be oot o a job." No, they wouldnae take us intae the war. So durin the war, the factory completely switched over tae war production, making engineerin parts, tank tracks, tank turrets an aw that. When we were doin the tank turrets, well, you know how a turret swivels? Well, we used tae have tae machine the facin bit, dae a groove in so they could get ball bearins in, you know, how a turret swivels round. Then I was on makin drums for – have you seen an aircraft carrier?[6] An that cable that goes across? [No, I haven't.] Well there's a drum at each side, it's part of the arrestin gear, which we would dae – it had a left-hand drum, an a right-hand drum – you see them doin it yet. Well, that cable was across when the plane came– I've not been on one either, but I take it there was a bolt right through, from the tail tae the engine block, an the tail-hook caught the cable, an these drums tightened it up, an that's how the aircraft gets slowed doon, so it didnae go over the end o the ship.

Having to remain at home as an essential worker did not, however, mean exemption from other wartime duties, such as service in the Home Guard or The Emergency Services. And so Bob joined The Auxiliary Fire Service (later renamed the National Fire Service). Though such a role may have seemed less dangerous than front-line combat, Kirkcaldy was a prime target, not only because it

[6] An aircraft carrier is a warship with a full-length flight deck. It serves as an airbase at sea as it has facilities for carrying, arming, deploying, and recovering aircraft.

was a major engineering centre but also because of its proximity to the Forth Rail Bridge and Rosyth Naval Base. Fire wardens were on round the clock alert for incendiary bombs, particularly after the Clydebank Blitz in 1941 when so many lost their lives in the line of duty.[7]

Jim Pratt was of the generation of children who began school at the start of the Second World War and for whom the school-leaving age was fourteen. In 1948 he applied to Melville-Brodie's for work, as he was keen on engineering – "I think it's in the blood," as he said:

> I'd just left school, young an innocent, an wanted tae go in for engineerin – it was good work, an good trainin, an I wanted tae be a fitter. When I started, Willie Black was there – he's one o the men that I remember, an I'm very pleased tae see him. Oh, Willie was a good man. An when I began, the take-home wage for an apprentice was twenty-one an nine-pence a week – £1-1s-9d.[8] An you'd take that home tae your Mum, oh, every penny of it! [laughs] Of course you'd get a wee bit back tae spend, mebbe thruppence, or somethin like that, but really, any money I needed, I got. An when my apprenticeship was finished, my wage was seven pounds fifteen an thruppence [£7-15s-3d[9]] after five years – that'd be in '53 or '54.

At the end of his apprenticeship he got a job in Edinburgh but when he decided to settle down and get married, he moved back to Fife to take up a job in Leven in September 1956. Despite the years between, Jim still looks upon his time with Melville-Brodie Engineering Company as the most important influence on his career, for it was there he was trained for the work he loved. The

---

7 Among the fire wardens called out was my grandfather, John Bennett, boilermaker at Blawarthill Hospital near the Clyde. For the rest of his life he was haunted by the horrors that fire wardens had to deal with in the aftermath of the Clydebank Blitz. (MB).

8 In today's currency, £1.09 a week.

9 £ 7.08.

Managing Director was Jock Brodie, who maintained the firm's work ethic, and though he had the reputation for being strict, the men had huge respect for him. Looking back, Jim recalled some of the incidents at work that still made him smile:

> I was in the blacksmith's shop one day an in came Mr. Brodie himself. An the blacksmith, he's standin lookin at somethin (the way you do, when you're concentrating). An Mr. Brodie says, "What d'you think you're supposed to be doing?"
>
> "Ehm, ehm," he says, kind of taken by surprise. An the apprentice, standin beside him, he could see that the blacksmith was just thinkin aboot the job, an he burst oot laughin! An Mr. Brodie turns an says tae this fellow an says, "An what are *you* supposed to be doing?"
>
> "Oh," he says, "I'm giein him a hand!"
>
> Another time Mr. Brodie came oot an I happened tae be passin, an I heard him talkin tae this bloke, an he was really gettin intae him. He was goin tae give him his books for standin aboot daein nothin! An the fellow says, "Well, that's OK, sir, you can gie me ma books if you like, but I don't work for you. I'm a lorry driver an I'm waitin on ma load!"

Bill Robertson, who grew up in Cardenden, also recalls the wartime years, though he was seventeen when he started at Melville-Brodie's. The first adjustment he had to make was to a change of name:

> Well, when I came here, there were four men called Willie an I was told, "Oh we cannae have any more o thae!" So they called me Bill. An everyone here (Kirkcaldy) knows me as Bill, even my wife, but when I go back tae Cardenden they caw me Willie. I started my apprenticeship in 1950, an the senior staff when I worked there, were Tam Simpson an Willie

> Williamson – he was the manager. But sadly, there's no many people left that I worked wi – they've gone… they've nearly aw died.

Bill worked in the drawing office, and though he's more likely to describe his skills in terms of "maist o us could draw on the back o a fag packet" he became a highly skilled draftsman. He had, and has, remarkable spatial ability and accurate recall, recently demonstrated when, in the absence of any photographs, he produced a drawing of the Melville-Brodie buildings for the front cover of this book. As far as Bill was concerned, however, that was just a sketch, compared to the requirements of the Melville-Brodie drawing office, where every minute detail had to be checked for accuracy by the senior draftsman. His approval gave the go-ahead to hand it over to the tracer, who made the final, permanent copy to be used by the pattern-makers and engineers, and eventually archived.

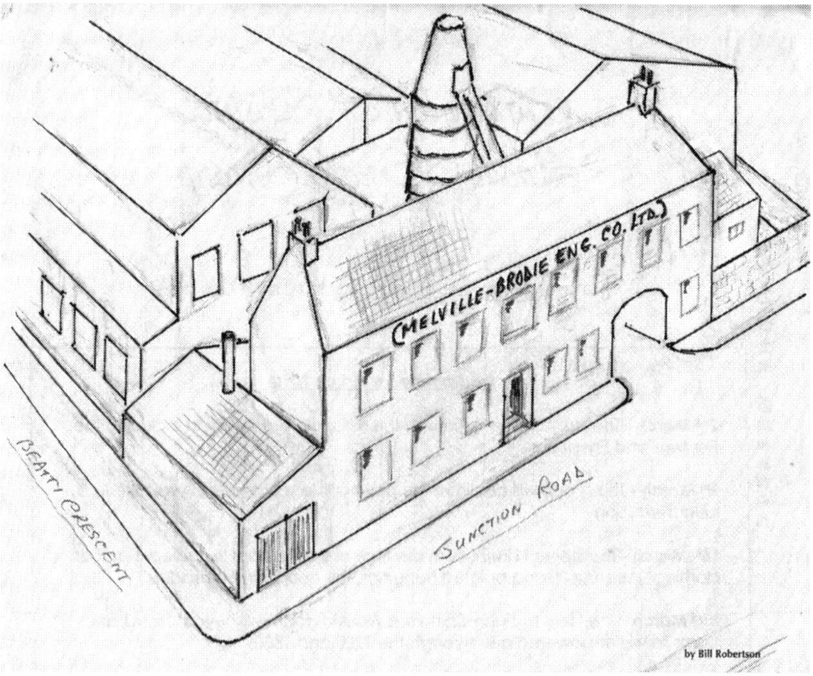

Bill Robertson's drawing of the Melville-Brodie building.

Apprenticeships in the Fifties and Sixties

As it was to be many years before the Scottish Education curriculum included 'Guidance' among the subjects, most school leavers relied on advice from family members or trusted friends. Angus (Gus) Robb, who left school in 1952, had been considering becoming a joiner, till his father helped him decide:

> My father spoke tae Willie Williamson that used tae be the manager, an, "Oh," he says, "he can start on Monday!" I was fifteen, an I'd just left school, an I served my apprenticeship there, an I was there for twenty-nine year. I was a fitter, an it was a good job. My father started serving his apprenticeship wi them, but he had this accident when he was only sixteen. He was in the machine shop, an when he was takin one o the belts over the shaft, he lost his arm. So that was him finished wi engineerin for good. So he was just sixteen, long afore he was married, so I never saw my Dad wi two airms. Of course he still had tae work after that, so instead o bein an engineer, he finished up in the dispatch room in Nairn's Linoleum Factory.

Despite his own misfortune, Mr. Robb retained the highest regard for Melville-Brodie's training, which, according to Gus, was 'second to none'.

Among the new generation who left school in the Fifties, are the 'boys' who have remained life-long friends ever since their time at Melville-Brodie's. The Department of Scottish Education had, by then, raised the school leaving age to fifteen, and so, as Dougie Reid explained, the starting age for apprentices also changed:

> Fifteen was the school leavin age then but you couldnae start your apprenticeship until you were sixteen, so you got yersel a job or somethin else. I always wanted tae dae somethin wi my hands – my father was a music teacher, but he didnae pay much

> attention tae me because I wasnae musically minded. I was interested in engineerin, an when I left school I was fortunate I passed the wee exam tae get into Kirkcaldy Technical College. So for that year, 15 tae 16, I was full-time there. There were classes in mathematics – that's essential if you're going work in engineerin, an of course the practical work. The technical college had sort o 'taster' sessions, when you were actually learnin aw different trades, like weldin, electrical, foundry work, carpentry, an aw that. So that year-long course gave me a wee bit of a springboard when it came tae startin work, because when employers were lookin for apprentices they went first tae the technical college, an then elsewhere.

And so began Dougie's time with Melville-Brodie Engineering Company:

> Oh, it was marvellous! The company was a total engineerin entity, in that it was all-embracin, an when you began the apprenticeship you got moved round the place – you did a wee bit of a stint in the pattern shop, you went up tae the mouldin shop, you went up tae the fittin, the grindin, the blacksmith. An besides that, you had tae dae three nights a week at night school. There was no day-release at that time – that began later on in my apprenticeship. So we'd get tae work at about seven tae light the fires then we started work at 7.30 an worked till 4, an then you rushed home tae get your tea so you'd be ready tae get tae night school from 7 tae 9. That was three nights a week, but later, they began this day-release scheme, when, instead of workin aw day, an then rushin off, which has tae be tirin, the system changed. An for firms whose workers were in the union, like Melville-Brodie, you'd go tae the technical college for a whole day, an you'd work full-time for the other

four. We were aw encouraged tae join the union – that was strong at Melville-Brodie's. That went back years, tae the start o the Second World War, an maybe before that. Bob Thomson could tell us there were two remaining craftsmen who were involved with the First World War – that was before his time, of course, but both wars affected Melville-Brodie's. It was durin the Second World War the government became more strict in the issuing of war work. From the government's point of view, they would make sure that a company had tae be absolutely certain tae be *bona fide,* that they were trade union organised, so there was no monkey business. They had learned from the experience durin the First World War, they had a lot o fly-by-nighters, an they were certainly no goin tae have it in the Second World War. It was a coalition government that was finally established, then the Labour members o parliament played a big, big part in that. An so Jock Brodie, who had taken over from his Dad at that time, came up tae the shop floor an told the men that, right reason or none, you had tae join the Union. Although the majority o people were in the union, it was not, what's termed, a 'closed shop' because there were some people of a religious denomination that said, "Oh, no, I'm a Mormon, or such like – I'm not allowed tae be a member of a union." But Jock Brodie said, "Well, allowed tae or not, you'll better join because we'll no get any war work if you don't join." An so, they aw had tae join a trade union. So it goes back before our time. It put everyone at Melville-Brodie's in a better position, an once your apprenticeship was finished, if you didnae end up with a good engineerin background there was something wrong.

When they applied to Melville-Brodie Engineering Company to be taken on as an apprentice, most of the boys had already decided which line of engineering they wanted to follow. For John Greig it was patternmaking, as he had a keen eye for design and its practical application to engineering. For this specialisation he would also have to prove his understanding of designs, plans and drawings (all two-dimensional) and demonstrate outstanding practical ability to think and operate in three dimensions, and in mirror images of drawings:

> There was the Drawing Office, the pattern shop, the fittin shop, an so on, an there was a variation in the rate of pay that went out to apprentices an tradesmen, although it may have been thruppence an hour. It was a kind of peckin order. But you made your choice based on what really interested you, an I wanted to be a patternmaker.
>
> A pattern, in engineering terms, is a replica made of wood or plastic or fibreglass or sometimes metal, an that replica is used to mass produce the end product, be it a camera casing, or an engine block, or part of the Forth Bridge. In the past, it was often made in wood: softwood if there was only a few to be made, hard wood if there were larger numbers, or in resin or metal if there were still larger numbers. An the apprenticeship at Melville-Brodie's was good training, because we used a wide range of appliances, an a wide range of material – timbers, yellow pines, an so on – an we dealt with a wide range of companies.
>
> The pattern was a full-size replica of the end product, so a patternmaker was party to a lot o goings-on prior to everybody else, because the draftsman would come through an say "Look, we're thinkin o designin that – is that feasible?" An it could be discussed in the pattern shop an decided whether or not it could be done, then it would be sent back an modified. An then the pattern has to be drawn to it, with a taper, so that, when it's eventually cast, it can come oot the sand.

Accuracy is the name of the game, and job satisfaction is one of the rewards. Teamwork is essential and, when the final copy of the drawing was approved, the tracer completed the process. The Melville-Brodie drawing office had one tracer, who, like all employees, was trained via a five-year apprenticeship.

In 1953, not long after she left school, fifteen year-old Maureen Griffiths began her career as a tracer at Melville-Brodie's. She had always been artistic, and her parents encouraged her to find a job that she would enjoy, preferably one where she could use her natural talent. Maureen recalls how they helped make her decision:

> My Mum came from the Borders. She was a tailoress from Galashiels and, growing up, I was always interested in sewing. So when I left school at fifteen, everybody was askin what was I going go do. There was a furrier's in Kirkcaldy at that time and, because I was interested in sewing, I went to an interview. But my Mum said, "All you'll get to do is make linings – for years, and years, and years you'll be making linings, but you'll never develop a fur coat!" [laughter] Anyway, on the weekend we went away down to Galashiels, because it was a festival time, and when we came back home we looked up the Fife Free Press, and there was this advert for a tracer in a drawing office. I was quite interested in drawing at school – I'd thought about staying on in school and doing Higher Art. And my Dad said, "Maybe you would like that?". So I went for the interview and I got the job, just like that, and I started the next month. And that was me for five years, doing my apprenticeship, from 1953, when I was fifteen, until I was twenty.
>
> Mr. Simpson, he was the boss, Tam Simpson, and the senior draftsman was Dave Griffiths – no relation. Then there was Mr. Simpson's son, Tom, Bill Robertson, Gordon Leitch and Gus McDonald – and me. All the draftsmen were better than me – well, they

> were older, and being the tracer meant that when they were satisfied that their drawing was the final one to be used, they'd hand it over to me, the tracer, so I'd make a more durable drawing on linen. They called it 'paper', thick paper, but it was really made of linen. A paper drawing wouldn't last, it would soon get damaged, so the tracer made the drawing that could be used repeatedly and also kept for posterity.

In Maureen's day, there were few jobs for women in an engineering company, and she found she was only girl in the drawing office, or on that particular floor:

> I was wi the boys! But we got on fine. Oh, they tease you and they can still do it! They can say something and I'm so naïve I just take it in and I'm easy led wi their jokes. I'm lucky, though, because I've got an easy-going nature, and so I take it all wi a pinch o salt. You'd have to, wi five boys in our drawing office, and Mr. Simpson, the boss, in his wee room. But downstairs in the front office there were two girls doing clerical work, as well as Miss Collins, who was Mr. MacKay's private secretary. He was the manager of the company and she was his P.A. – Winnie was her first name, though we always called her Miss Collins – and she was, oh, so old-fashioned, wi her white hair scraped back in a bun at the back o her head. She was always well-dressed, always smart, though so were the girls, as well as we could afford. I remember we had a lot to do with Miss Collins – she stayed in Douglas Street in Kirkcaldy, and she was there for years, and years, and years. I think she was in wi the bricks! I still remember Wilma Reid and Mary Gilliard who worked in the office, and I still keep in touch with Mary though she lives in Canada.

In the drawing office everyone used high-quality instruments, so Maureen soon bought her own set: "I still have them, all in their boxes. It was Riefler instruments I had, just a wee box, wi my drawin pen, my set-square, and everything." As with any apprenticeship, there was a lot to learn, so from the day she began, Maureen kept a notebook of all the tasks she was given. Each job had specific requirements with new terminology to take in, so Maureen kept notes and made sure she kept up with everything: "Ye just took it in your stride. You were young and when they said that's what ye had to do, you just had to learn how to do it all." Years later she is reminded of drawings that she traced: "I look at my notebook and remember my very first drawing I did – it was the sluice on the Lochty Burn!" She learned that a sluice is part of an artificial passage for water to flow through, with a gate for controlling the flow. From time to time, a news item reminds her of drawings that she traced, such as the 2015 announcement of the closure of Scotland's last paper mill:

> We made paper-making machines at Melville-Brodie's, and a lot of it went up to Tullis Russell's where they did all that the paper printing. I worked on the drawins and did the tracins. So when it was being built, with the big towers and that, I'd watch it getting built and I'd say "That's what my drawing was!" When you hear the news that it's closing, it brings it back to you. It's so sad.

Besides the techniques of tracing, Maureen's job also entailed printing, a process which has long since been taken over by computers. As she had to learn to use chemicals and inks it made sense to Maureen to protect her clothes:

> I used to have that floral overall on all the time, because when you were working wi chemicals, wi splashes or anything like that, you had to be careful. It was just to keep your own clothes clean because you were leaning over a board, and when you put

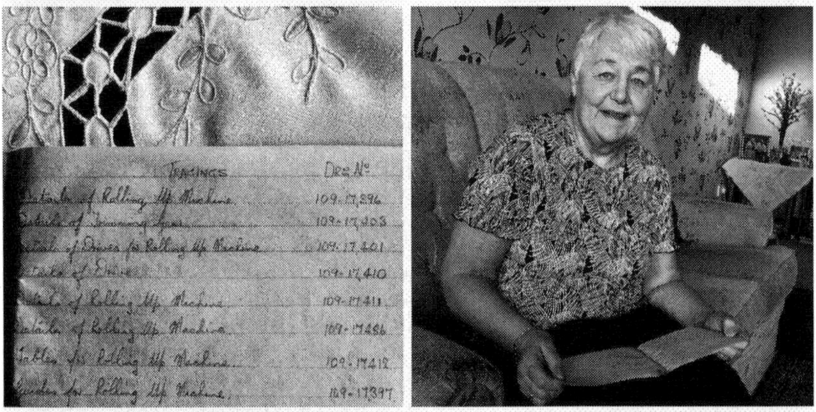

Top: Maureen Griffiths and her drawing instruments.

Middle: "I still have my wee notebook… I kept it after I got married and I still have it!" (Maureen Shaw at home in Glenrothes, 2016.)

Bottom: Maureen shows one of the engineering drawings, with a close-up of the intricate detail entailed.

> the tracing paper on, if it was tracing you were doing, and you'd to chalk it all, because if you didn't chalk it, your ink wouldn't stick to it. So that's how the ink went to it, because you took the surface off the linen. Now, if you'd seen this printing machine – there was a round arc about five feet tall wi a glass panel in front, and my tracing, I would put it on, put the printing paper on top, close it, and then we had this arc lamp and I used to pull it up and down [Maureen demonstrates with wide arm movements] and this is what printed; this is what made our prints – that was the light shining on it to make it print. And you had to learn how to do it and not shine it on too long in the same spot or it wasnae any good, so you'd go up and down, and back and forth [arm movements to demonstrate] until it was all printed. And then when I got the blue print, they had a big bath, a metal bath, and you used to put it in, and put solutions in, run the water on it, and then hang them up to dry in a big cupboard – it was heated, but not very hot, and you put the drawings over wooden rails.

Once dried, it was over to the pattern-shop, which was just "through on the landing, where the pattern-makers worked, and if anything went wrong they just come through. And," she added, "I did the First Aid (with no previous training) as well as all the printing."

When Maureen began her apprenticeship the foreman of the pattern-shop was Alex (Eck) Morgan, who later took on John Greig as his new apprentice. The rigorous training began by teaching him that every stage of a job had to be carried out to the highest standards before it would be ready for the next part of the operation. John found the whole process inspiring, and when presented with a drawing was all set for a new challenge:

> When we'd make the pattern, it would go down to the foundry to be moulded an cast, an to be cored to make

it hollow, an so on. The patternmaker would supply core boxes to hollow oot the castin an machinin allowance, because every stage o production had to work together – they had the turners an so on, and flanges, so it could be bolted together. It had to be tapered, so it could be drawn oot o the mould cleanly, without fallin in on itself, an the corners had to be round, an filleted, so the cast metal could flow an run. It all had to be planned, so the castin would work, an be sound. Molten metal contracts, an it shrinks quite a bit, an every metal contracts differently – brass, aluminium, steel, iron – so, for each pattern you had to know what it was bein made for, so you could add the contraction allowance. An the contraction allowance had to be calculated in every case, as they maybe had to produce three or four sizes, an each pattern could be a different size, dependin on what it was being made for – brass or aluminium or cast iron. So all these details had to be taken into consideration. There was a lot o satisfaction in the trade. An then once it was made, you had the pride o paintin the pattern, makin it look good. Then it went down to the foundry to be cast – we used to joke, an say you took it to the foundry be destroyed, but that's a bit harsh! When it went down to the foundry it was put into use, an of course it got a lot o brute force, hammerin an thumpin an shakin around. We made patterns for paper mills, silk mills, linen mills, linoleum factories, such as Nairn's, and Barry, Ostlere & Shepherd's in Kirkcaldy, an we had the patterns for Tullis Russell, the paper mills in Fife. And once a pattern was used, it was put into the Pattern Store, and a record kept. Melville-Brodie's had four large pattern stores, an that's where we kept patterns for twenty-five years before we scrapped them.

Dougie's inspiration was in the Machine Shop where he would become a turner, and he recalls his excitement in getting ready to begin his five-year apprenticeship:

> Before I started, I had tae get a boilersuit.[10] A shop in Kirkcaldy did them, Sharps, on the High street, near the Port Brae. This was the firm made aw the boilersuits, because Kirkcaldy has a tremendous linen industry – we could tell you more about that, but that's another story. They were navy-blue, no thon bright blue you see now, an they cost thirty bob. It seemed like a lot o money, though that boilersuit lasted you for a long time, unless you grew. Like Willie says, you always got a long one, an you tucked the sleeves up, but I soon found oot I had tae have more than one!
>
> I remember my first day at work. We started at seven in the mornin, an there you were, waitin at the doors tae go in. An everythin was new, an you were neat an tidy, an you werenae too sure if you got the right boilersuit! I'd had gotten an all-in-one, which I thought was the right thing. But on my very first day, I kept seein boys, an they were in dungarees, an there were others wi different things, a jacket an so on. An I'm there thinkin, "Have I got the right thing on?"

Unbeknown to Dougie, he wasn't the only one who felt apprehensive for, no matter which line an apprentice wanted to follow, his initial concern was that he would start off on the right foot. John agreed it was much the same in the pattern-shop:

> My first day must have been similar tae Dougie's, but we just had tae wear a bib an tucker, ordinary dungarees. I was both excited an apprehensive, but the biggest worry for the patternmakers was investing in tools.

[10] The OED, 1928, lists boilersuit, though it is often as written boiler suit or boiler-suit.

The fitting shop boys also wore boilersuits and, like the rest of the apprentices, Bill Simpson and Gus Robb soon got used to the weekly routine:

> Oh they weren't supplied, you'd tae buy it, an Mum had tae wash it. When you went in on a Monday it was aw nice an clean, but by Friday it was manky. You took it home every Friday, aw fu o grease an aw thing, but in the latter days you used tae get it done at the work. I don't remember that so it must have been after my time – these boys were mollycoddled!

If new apprentices were looking for reassurance or encouragement from the boys who started a year or two ahead of them, they could be sorely disappointed. They were much more likely to find themselves among pastmasters of the wind-up trade, senior apprentices who enjoyed testing the mettle of the new boys. Yet it was in this very setting that began friendships, which have endured over fifty years.

Among them was Drew Sneddon, still capable of remaining deadpan while he looks the novice straight in the eye and sets his sights on some hilarity. And he should know what it's like, for, having discovered that, to follow his real ambition, he had to be tough enough to change from one apprenticeship course to another:

> Before I left the school, I'd decided I wanted tae go into engineerin 'cause my father was an engineer – a *good* engineer. He was a mechanical engineer, an he was one o the best. He was wi the Coal Board at the time, as an engineer, an in his line o work he went tae Melville-Brodie's tae give them contracts for the NCB work [National Coal Board]. He knew they were the best, so, in some ways, my father chose Melville-Brodie, but I *wanted* tae go there anyway because he'd told me about it many, many times. I went tae the Technical College in Kirkcaldy first, an I was sixteen

> when I started work. But before I got an opening at Melville-Brodie's, I started in Balfour's in Leven, an I lost my finger the day I was leavin. That happened on the Friday, an I started on the Monday at Melville-Brodie's. So, I started in the drawin office, where I did about a year an a half – you learned how tae use the slide rule an aw that. I was the junior, an these guys had the real expertise. An though I enjoyed it, I realised that wasn't really for me. So I decided tae change, an I went tae the fittin shop tae complete my apprenticeship as a fitter – that's what I really wanted.

New apprentices soon learned there were times when it was better to keep silent and watch, rather than confront someone, who, by comparison, had the confidence of a battle-hardened warrior. Matthew Morrison remembers being puzzled by what seemed to him to be a peculiarity, yet he opted not to question the journeyman or older apprentices, as he had already seen the potential for pranksters:

> There was guy who worked wi us, an at the back o where he worked, there was a wee shelf at the back o his machine, an there was all sorts o paper, an foil on this shelf – cigarette papers, aw sorts o papers, tissues and foil, cut into one-inch squares. An I wondered what was all this for, but I was frightened to ask because they'd just take the mickey. Until one day, the guy was setting up his machine, which was on a big flat table, an of course it has to be level, absolutely spot on, so he got one o this, an one o that, and he just levered up one corner to level it! That's why he kept aw the wee bits o paper![11]

Fortunately, among the journeymen were teachers, such as Willie Black, who were to become the role models for a new generation

[11] The thickness of one popular brand of cigarette paper is 0.05 mm, which is less than 0.0019 of an inch.

of engineers. First impressions can be the most lasting, as Dougie remembers when he first set eyes on the turner at work: "Talk about skill! If you'd seen Willie Black at the lathe, it was absolutely marvellous!"

Willie had similar memories of Bob Thomson as an instructor, and likewise, Bob could look back to his role model when he began in 1935:

> I think Willie Williamson was a right psychiatrist. He knew how tae teach people. He would talk you into daein things that you'd probably think, "I'd never dae that!" But you'd dae it. Oh, it was quite a place, an it became your whole life, really. We were just talkin about how it influences other areas o your life. You were workin tae very precise measurements – you had the callipers, an you had rules, an you'd make a thing the dimensions maybe 9.352 inches, an you'd get near that with a rule, precise, an you thought you had it, an you said tae the foreman, "Right," an he come with the micro wire an checked it an told you, "You're two-thousandths too much!" Or he'd say, "one-thou too much. Take it off!" Less than a hair's breadth because we worked tae tenths o a thou.[12] I was there for eighteen years – I started in 1935, an I left in 1953, after I was married. We had a wee hoose near the works, an then we had a wee girl. So we got a new hoose, a cooncil hoose, but it was two miles away, an you couldnae get a bus, you had tae walk. So I walked, February, March, April, these three winter months, an it was too much. So I got the chance o this other job oot the town. But Melville-Brodie's didnae want me tae go – they tried tae stop me in fact! An the firm that I got the job with was Kinghorn Bottleworks, which was at one time just a wee bottle-works. But

[12] A 'thou' is the term used by engineers to denote 0.001 of an inch. In terms of accuracy, Melville-Brodie engineers worked to one-tenth of a thou. (The 'th' is pronounced as in 'think'.)

> at that time it was part o DCL,[13] which was aw the bottle-works in the country, United Glass, bottle manufacturers. So the manager said the job was mine, workin wi the machinery there, as a turner, because they needed a lot o turnin done. In fact I was only there a year when I was made charge-hand, then as time went on I was made foreman.
>
> Eventually there was a job come up that I fancied, teachin apprentices, so I went up for that job an got it. That was for a group-trainin scheme in Kirkcaldy, called Fifeshire Engineering Training Scheme. It was based just behind the station in Oriel Road, an we were takin 120 boys a year, trainin apprentices. I was there for seven years so I must have trained a good thousand anyway! Then, after I was away, retired, they changed the name tae Oriel Training Services – it moved tae Glenrothes, then folded.

One of the great satisfactions for such highly-skilled men was their success in passing on their skills to new generations. And, as any good teacher should know, subject expertise is not what makes the learning experience enjoyable; it is the ability to pass on that knowledge with clarity, patience and a sense of humour. The journeyman and apprentice develop a bond of trust and friendship that endures for life, such as Bob and Willie, man and boy, who are now in their nineties. And so also with Willie and the 'boys' he trained, not only the ones who became turners, but also those who specialised in other areas. The apprentice had to understand the interconnectedness of every stage and, in aiming for a career in engineering, he could only reach his highest potential by discovering the area best suited to his own aptitude and skill. For some sixteen-year-olds, the choice was not an instant decision, as Matthew Morrison recalled:

> I started as an apprentice turner in 1959 an Willie Black was one o my journeymen. You hear a lot o

[13] DCL (Distillers Company Limited), which later became UDV and Diageo.

> people sayin that journeymen didnae really pass on their skills, you know, because they didnae want you tae get better than them, or get more money or anythin! Willie was the opposite – unforgettable. Then after four years I went into the drawin office, an progressed tae bein a designer. It was a very good trainin – the best.

For others, Willie was both teacher and mentor throughout their time at Melville-Brodie's. Dougie can still picture him at work:

> If you'd seen him at the lathe! Oh, Willie was definitely good with his hands, he definitely was, but more importantly, he had tae be good with his brain. An he was also good at puttin his trade across, because I learned an immense amount from him, an men like him. It was a great experience. An oh, the banter! You would be daein quite a lot o jobs – say, machinin screws, an things like that, an once you're learned how tae dae it, it would be fairly quick an operation. An then the likes o Willie would come doon an say, "Where are you stackin them?" You'd say, "I've only done that," (pointin tae the few you'd managed), an he'd say, [joking] "Oh come on, you've gotta dae more than that! I've got tae get ma bonus offa that!" Oh, there were some good laughs!
>
> It was a great place tae work. I remember my first pay packet was thirty bob – it was a ten-shilling note an a one-pound note. I can still picture the wage packet: the top corner was open, an the corner o the pound note an the ten bob note stuck oot, so you could count the right notes were there. An my Granny got aw that money, because this was the thing in my family, that the first pay packet that a grandchild got, you gave it tae your Granny. That was tradition, an the thing was, it didnae matter that my boilersuit cost me 30 bob!

To begin with, most o the boys walked tae work, but as soon as you could, you got a bicycle – no a new one, but anythin you could get your hands on, even just a frame or bits, an you could put one together. I mind Willie's bike when I started, because the frame was actually from a lady's bike, it didnae have a crossbar – not that it mattered, but you just notice these things.

The apprentices didnae have much money, an neither did the men, but in those days everybody smoked. An some people used tae pick up dog-ends! But we had a lad, an he was worse than a lot o folk at pickin up the dog-ends. Someone would drap a fag, an there would be a couple o good puffs in it. So this day, we got in ahint this big electrical cabinet, an we'd laced this fag wi thread, an we laid it on the floor where he couldnae miss it. But where we were hidin, there wasnae room for us aw, so I was lyin on the bottom, an there was 3 or 4 guys on top o me, an when this lad put his hand down tae get the dog-end it wisnae there because we kept pullin it further until we started tae laugh! An the rest o them got oot the road quick, an I was stuck at the bottom, an he come round an got hud o me an hammered me! But I couldnae dae nothin for laughin! Mind, though, I got that boy back, but I'm no gonnae tell ye how I did it! Oh, the things we got up to!

An I used tae smoke Senior Service until one o Willie's pals said, "I wouldnae smoke them! I wouldnae smoke Senior Service – you ken, every packet o Senior Service, there's tuppence goes tae the Pope. So fae then on I never smoked Senior Service! It wasnae that there was any sectarianism, because there wasn't; you were young, an they just knew how tae wind you up.

Most of the apprentices and journeymen were on first-name terms, though Mr. Brodie was always Mr. Brodie. Maureen recalled his occasional visits to the drawing office:

> He was the boss, of course, so he was Mr. Brodie, and you had to look up to him. Oddly enough, when he wasnae there, the girls always referred to him as John Brodie. He came to the office no very often, but everything had to be spruced up and just right when Mr. Brodie came. Miss Collins made sure of that. He was pleasant enough, he would only say 'Hello', but I didn't have much to do with him. Miss Collins was the one.

As a rule, the apprentices all respected their elders, though now and again they couldn't resist testing the boundaries, even when they sensed a level of risk. Bill Simpson, who began the same year as Dougie, was among the spirited youngsters who spent his life pushing the boundaries, despite discovering the consequences:

> See, if you were a cheeky apprentice, the journeyman would take you, an he'd get a handfu o grease, an put it on your privates! That was standard procedure if you were cheeky tae *certain* journeyman! They'd grease your private parts – well, they'd grease your balls, an that's what they called it!

No sooner had Bill described the procedure, when, true to form, Drew confirmed the incident with, "Aye, but in his case, they tried, but they couldnae find them!" Banter is the name of the game, yet nobody misses the original goal, as Drew immediately picks up again, making sure he leaves the impression that matters most:

> But it was perfect trainin, it really was. I was 21 when I finished, an I could hold my hand tae anybody else, believe you me – except Bill, I accept that. But

> honestly, it was a nice place tae work, it really was, an there was a work ethic tae go with it. It was like a family, working there, because you might have people that you fell oot wi, then five minutes after that, it'd be fine, an that was it! But we could tell you stories!

Bill, who had a long career as a fitter, has plenty, both hilarious and serious:

> I'll tell you a story – for comparison, like when you start work an you find yourself among engineers from aw over the place. When I finished my time at Melville-Brodie's, I went tae the Merchant Navy. An soon afterwards, I joined a ship, an it was terrible – the state the ship was in. An the minute we got tae the dry docks in London, on the Thames, the engine packed up. An there's a thing caw'd the cross-head bearings packed up – an then when we were in the middle o the Atlantic we had tae replace it. An the Second Engineer was there, an there was ball-bearins tae be scraped in, an he says tae me, "Can you scrape that in?" I says, "Aye, I can dae that," so I got the job. Then when he saw me in action, ever after that, if there was cross-head bearins tae be scraped in, then I got the job. An I was the *junior* engineer. An that was Melville-Brodie's trainin. You could go anywhere in the world wi that kind o trainin. An we did.

Apprentices all had to be good at mathematics, able to read drawings and to demonstrate exceptional spatial ability and three-dimensional skills. Among the boys were several who were mathematically gifted and the journeymen liked nothing better than to test them at every opportunity. The apprentices themselves enjoyed a challenge, as Dougie recalled:

> Some o the journeymen who were teachin us used

tae pose questions tae us. An they would think up mathematical questions for us, an we'd aw try tae work them oot – oh, you wouldn't want them tae get the better o you! An in those days, we were aw space buffs because the first rocket had just reached the moon an everybody was talkin aboot Yuri Gagarin. We used tae buy the *Eagle Magazine* an *Dan Dare,* an aw that kin' o thing. We'd want tae find out, an we'd be talkin aboot this, an everything.
[Dougie turns to Bob]

An you mind Aund Farr? [Bob: "Oh yes."] We caw'd him 'Aund', short for Andrew. Well, he had a high reputation at Melville-Brodie's, because he'd been overseas, an that, an we knew he was quite worldly-wise, you see. So we listened a wee bit more intently tae what Aund had tae say, because he must ken – he'd been roun the world, you know! So this day, when we'd aw been talkin about Gagarin, he brought us aw thegither an he says, "Right, aw you space whizz kids! Right, noo, I want you tae find this oot: What's the inverted angle o the – ?" An he names a small delicate part o the female anatomy, which none o us boys had ever heard o! We'd never heard the word! Well, we were dumfounded. So we went intae aw sorts o debatin circles, an aw the rest o it. An o course, Aund Farr an Willie Black an them, they were roarin an laughin, watchin us. An they kept this goin for weeks an weeks an weeks! Nae internet then tae find oot! An you wouldnae go an *ask* anybody, you had tae try an find oot. An when it dawned on us! Oh! They were unbelievable some o the things they told us! But on that occasion, we werenae expectin anything like that, 'cause mostly it was relatively clean-funny.

Not every apprentice made the grade, however, and no matter how enthusiastic they might have been when they began, that alone was not enough. Willie had an eye for aptitude, skill and meticulous attention to detail. Nothing less would do, and no matter how keen the boy might be, if he didn't measure up, as Willie explained, the only thing to do was to end the apprenticeship in the kindest possible way:

> Well, when we started apprentices, maybe three or four o them, aw about sixteen or seventeen, whatever they were doin you could see if there was one o them – an you'd know, that boy was goin home an havin his tea, what have you, an his Mum would maybe say, "How are you gettin on at work?" An whatever he'd say tae his Mum, you knew he wouldnae want tae upset her. Then you knew that he'd be goin oot with his pals, an maybe they'd know he wasnae managin so well, an that that was always in his mind, "I've tae go back there tomorrow." An I used tae feel sorry for them, because I knew the laddie, an I'd know how he'd feel. An I'd say, "You know, son, you've a five year apprenticeship, an if you're at this trade till you're sixty-five – think aboot it!" So I'd speak tae the boy, an I'd say, "I feel sorry for you." An I might know the boy's mother, an I had this idea o how he was doin, I used tae tell them, "You know, you'd be better tae get your son another job." If the boy wanted tae stay on, I says, "Oh no – you'd be better packin it in." An he would be.

Relying on advice from an experienced journeyman was the best thing an apprentice could possibly do. Ronnie Fleming, who began a year later than Dougie, remembers the advice he got on the day he applied for his apprenticeship in Melville-Brodie's foundry:

> Willie just mentioned you shouldnae dae jobs that didnae suit, jobs you didnae like – well, when I started, I'd never heard o a moulder before, but trades were pretty scarce on the ground. I was oot in Cardenden,

> which is six miles oot, an being from a coal minin village, o course, like everyone else I applied go tae the pit, but I failed my medical on eyesight. An then, when I heard they're lookin for an apprentice moulder up at Melville-Brodie, I said, "That'll do!" So I went up tae see it, an the old gaffer started me, Bob Williamson. An I was the last apprentice he started. He smoked a cigarette oot the corner o his mooth because he'd been tae America, an he used tae talk aboot this friend in America, Boston Bill. So when I got there, Bob Williamson looked at me an he said, "Oh yi want tae be a moulder eh? I cannae say it's the best trade in the world, but you've come tae the best place tae learn it!" he says.

As the foundry needed a constant supply of metal, there was a large yard with a separate entrance. To the average passer-by, it may have looked like a scrap-yard without cars, but John and Dougie remember its importance to everyone who worked there:

> This whole yard was full o scrap metal wi a crane, an a separate gated entry for a vehicle. An the crane used tae work in this area breakin the scrap, droppin the big, five-ton load on it –like a huge ball, they ones they used when they knocked down the tenements. So there was a gaffer, the manager of the foundry, Bob Williamson who was in charge o makin sure the metal was aw right. He wasnae a chemist or anythin, he just knew by lookin at the scrap that was bought in, an he knew which metal was needed for a job. It was aw ferrous, it was aw iron an, for example, if you were makin engineerin castins, it was simple, the metal had tae be from some kind o machinery, like lathes an old millin machines. The scrap lorry would come in, an he wouldn't tip his scrap until our gaffer saw it. He would look in, an if it was just a load o auld rhone pipes, he'd say, "No, no, that's no use tae us,

> take that doon tae Johnny Leitch, an he'll use it." An there it could be used for makin more rhone pipes, an manhole covers. An doon the road at Leitch's Foundry, where they made toby lids, these weren't machined, so the iron didnae need tae be anythin in particular. But our gaffer would make sure we had the right metal for the foundry boys.

Few got to know 'the right metal' better than Ronnie:

> I was fifteen when I started in the foondry but you didnae start your apprenticeship immediately – you were just the boy boiling the drums – the tin cans for making the tea. Well, the foundry was completely different from the rest o the places – an as far as aw the rest o them were concerned, it was the bottom o the heap, right through the hierarchy, from the drawin office, on doon. They'd say, if you didnae make it there, you got put doon tae the fittin shop; if you couldnae make it at the fittin shop you got put tae the turnin shop, the lathes an that; if you couldnae make it there, it was the smiddy, the blacksmith; an then if you couldnae make it there, an aw through the way you got threatened, "You're gonna finish up in the foundry! If you dinnae buck up you're gonna tae finish up in the foundry!" That was what they used tae threaten the apprentices with, for next tae coal minin it was the worst job, a terrible job.

At the end of each day, Willie remembered that, "When these boys were ready tae go home at night they were black, just absolutely filthy!" But, as Ronnie added, there was some compensation for being covered with dust and grime from head to foot:

> We got extra money for the workin conditions, we were the highest paid, though you were absolutely filthy! Ye came oot at night like a coal miner! An we

> had one shower for twenty-five folk, but aw the big journeymen got in first. Aw the same, the miners down in Cardenden were much better off than we were – they had a wee bit mair money than farm workers, so they had motor bikes an they could go up tae Stanley. We'd be lucky if we could get an old bicycle. An in the foundry the older journeyman used tae tell us, "Stupid trade this, you'll never make any money at this trade! You'd be better bein a painter or a plumber, where you could dae work at night, dae homers."

An apprentice moulder had to be physically fit and strong, and willing to work in uncomfortable extremes of temperatures, with all the hazards of dust and noise, and constant risk of burns and other injuries. In these challenging conditions Ronnie soon learned that total focus and concentration were crucial at every stage. If an apprentice moulder were to build up self-confidence, however, he had to have the inner strength to ignore insinuations about low prestige attached to the job, for prestige is not measured in terms of comfort and conditions.

> You don't become a moulder for pleasure! Like I said, workin in an iron foundry was, next tae coal minin, the worst job in the world – it could be absolutely terrible, just a *horrible* job. When they were castin it was awful hot, but in the winter it was awful cold, because there was so much iron, boxes, an the whole floor was just damp mouldin sand, about ten feet deep. An it was aw old, it never changed, an they never modernised it from Victorian times. In fact the big crane we had in the foundry came from the buildin o the Forth Rail Bridge, the big wooden crane.
>
> They were old fashioned, but at Melville-Brodie's a lot o that worked tae your advantage. For example, they got in pneumatic rammers for rammin the sand, an these pneumatic rammers were certainly a

> lot quicker, but oh, the noise! So you said, "Oh no, they're too noisy!" An they'd go back tae the old way, usin various rammers.

No such consideration was given to the workforce that was just through the wall from Melville-Brodie's. The 'boys' remembered how this 'modernisation' affected them:

> The Fife Forge Company used tae have steam hammers in their forge, an when they were goin, the noise was such that the whole o Kirkcaldy heard the hammerin! You could hear it aw over the toon, an we were right next tae them, just through the wall! An sometimes at Melville-Brodie's when we were machinin things, an you'd have tae dae this very carefully trying tae work tae a thousandth o an inch, suddenly Fife Forge would decide, "We're gonna start hammerin!" The noise was bad enough, but this affected what we'd be doin – you'd feel it through your machine, because every machine was constructed into the earth, on big wooden beams – it gave you a bit o fluidity, a bit o ease o vibration, but it also picked up vibration. An in the pattern-shop too, when these steam-hammers started, oh, the noise! An the tools we were usin would vibrate an it would show through onto the metal – oh aye, those big machines could seriously affect everyone.

Preferring not to use pneumatic rammers at Melville-Brodie's, the foundry workers continued with the older method of flattening sand.

> When you were usin one o these auld rammers, you couldnae have too big a face on it, for if you formed a flat (as we'd say), an you put more sand on it – it wouldnae stick tae it. You know how you see a plasterer or a cement worker, they put one layer on,

an then they score it aw for the next layer tae stick? If you caused a flat, that sand could actually pass away, so the head o the rammer would move, maybe an inch by two inches, an these big boxes were aw divided into small boxes, an you had tae ram each individual one. An the apprentices, they had tae riddle the sand, an that's another thing – they had riddlin machines, an they made up some excuse that it was bad for strippin the clay content oot o the sand. So nope, back tae hand-riddlin! An you got two on a shovel, an we made up a game, tae try an stop the riddler! You wouldnae riddle sand aw day, oh no, not aw day! As they moved up through their apprenticeship they may get a shot on the shovel, while the apprentice under you would be riddlin away. Among the apprentices there was a hierarchy, a skill level. I remember in my third year, Bert Lindsay, a fantastic moulder, but a big bully o a man – he was ex-army, he was always moaning, he'd had some malaria. An we used tae use gaggers an hingers[14], an he says, "Right Ronnie, go an get the gaggers an hingers for this job an I'll put them in." An I says, "No Bert, we'll *both* go an get the gaggers an hingers, an we'll *both* put them in."

"You impudent little bugger!" he says, an then, "What year are you in?"

An I says, "Third."

An he said, "Well, you're maybe right enough."

There was a knack in puttin them in, these hingers. The sand actually hung fae them, an I've see the sand hingin 18 inches, an if you put a hinger in that way, you'd put one at the opposite angle tae counteract it. An these boxes had tae be lifted, put down, turned over, an then finished off, an turned back, an put back

[14] See, John F. Buchanan, *Foundry Nomenclature: the Moulder's Pocket Dictionary*, (London & New York, 1903). HANGERS. pieces of iron for carrying the weight of projecting or depending parts of a mould. (GAGGERS: pieces of iron embedded in the sand of a mould to keep it intact. GAGGERING. The method of setting gaggers.

in. There was a skill tae it. But then they introduced modern methods, which was CO_2, which was just ordinary silica sand mixed with sodium silicate, an you put a series o holes in it. an injected CO_2 gas into it an that hardened it. So you could more or less dae anythin you liked with it, whereas the old style, green sand, you'd tae be very careful, an very gentle with it.[15]

An you were runnin aboot wi a hundredweight o molten metal in the wee ladles. An they had a shank, a long shank, the other end was split into trams that someone carried, an the floor was anythin but even. Then you'd be pourin this metal into the mould an going back, an gettin more oot the big ladle. An if you started tae shake a wee bit, the journeyman would ask: "What were you doing last night?" But it was the camaraderie o the moulders too, you know. Like coal minin, when you were castin you had tae trust the boys on the ladle – don't dae anythin stupid wi the molten iron.

An as you can imagine in the foundry, wi molten iron gaun aw ower the place, you used tae get wee sparks, but in my time nobody was ever seriously burnt. But there were accidents – like the tragedy in the machine shop with the chap MacArthur.

[15] Green sand is the term used for damp sand. (Not dry sand.)

Bill Robertson standing beside a new part for paper making-machinery, inside the end bay of the fitting shop. Melville-Brodie Engineering Co, c. 1968.

THE APPRENTICES: Matthew Morrison photo collection.

The apprentices beside a horizontal lathe, 1959. Back row: Sandy Pennycuick, Sandy Picket, Dougie Reid. Front row: Eddie Murdoch (Sammy), Ronnie Fleming, Bill Simpson, John (Jock) MacMillan. [MM]

The boys in boilersuits. From left: Bill Cunningham (Tipper), Dougie Reid, Mathew Morrison (Matt) and Eddie Murdoch (Sammy), c. 1958.

Back row: Sandy Pennycuik, Ronnie Fleming, John McMillan (Jock), Sandy Picket and Eddie Murdoch. Front: Bill Simpson & Dougie Reid, 1958.

Journeymen craftsmen. Inscription on the back is: 'Senior brotherhood just prior to the one trouser leg being raised, 1959.' Front left: Sharma, Tom Cramey, Willie Black, Tom Patterson and Andrew (Aund) Farr. [MM]

Mary Gilliard sitting at Maureen Griffiths' desk in the Drawing Office, mid-1950's.

Apprentices' night out. From Left: Dougie Reid, Bill Simpson, Eddie Murdoch (Sammy), Eck Murray and Sandy Pennycuick, 1960. [MM]

Staff of the Drawing Office 1950's: Gordon Leitch (back), Gus MacDonald (L), Maureen Griffiths in her floral overall, and Bill Robertson (R).

Health and Safety

As the safety of the workforce is of prime importance, risk assessment is essential to all areas of engineering. Occasionally, when local newspapers reported some horrific accident that shocked the town, everyone in Kirkcaldy became aware of the dangers of working in a factory.[15] From the outset, apprentices were trained to observe codes of safety, particularly as it applied to their own area of specialisation. In the history of the firm there were very few fatalities, but the boys still heard about them from journeymen such as Willie, who remembered:

> The Techy shop put the gantry up, the long jib, an it was bolted – the four bolts, you know these big beams they had in the machine shop, an they had it bolted across. That was fixed – or so they thought, and an H-beam. An they put their jib in – the one that goes back an forward. Well, they were liftin this big pipe – about five or six o them aw tryin tae manoeuver it in, or takin it out. An does the jib where it was bolted no dae a dunner – one o the bolts gave way. Snap! An down it came! Well I wasn't in the area o the accident - I was at work when it happened, but I didnae see the accident. It just so happened Dave MacArthur was pushin it in, there were a liner up, he pushed it in, an he must have lost his balance, an he fell an the thing came down on him. Oh it was a tragedy!

Occasionally there were minor accidents, and those who learned from an early experience were the most convincing teachers. Like the rest of the boys in his year, Dougie paid close attention,

---

[15] For example, in William M. Melville's time, there was a horrific accident in the Denfield Linen Works, directly across the road from Melville & Hendersons. A young woman, who lived and worked in Sinclairtown, caught her hair in one of the machines and was completely scalped. The accident no doubt affected all the whole community as well as the factory, which was owned by J. Main & Sons. The headline in the *Dundee Courier* read 'Has Her Hair and Scalp Torn Off'. (Feb. 21, 1911).

recalling that "the men were quite good at telling us, no this rigid regime for Health & Safety, but it was common sense, to tell you to watch your hands an your hair and things like that." And, as Willie added, "Aye, an no muck aboot with the rules."

When he was in his mid-teens, Willie, like most youngsters, assumed that accidents only happen to other people. Pointing to his own hand, however, he recalled the experience that changed his opinion as well as the shape of a thumb:

> I would only be there about a year, when I lost the top o it, but it was partly my fault because I took the guard off the back o the machine. We were doin the bolts for the tubs, a right-hand screw an a left-hand screw, an you had tae go tae the back o the lathe tae reverse it. An Black had his guard off – thinkin you could dae it quicker an make more, because the job was on piecework! An where I was standin, I must have slipped, an my hand went in the gear wheels an just, oh! Quick as a flash, see, an juggled a bit off. An I had tae go doon tae the hospital – oh wait the noo, was it Christmas Day or a Boxing Day? Anyway it was one o the two. An when I get there, mark now, I'm sittin in there wi a big bandage on – I could always remember gettin taken in tae have it sorted. An their operatin place was just a small room – an then the Sister, she came an said, "Look at the state o your hand!"
>
> An I said, "Well, it *has* tae be dirty! I've been workin aw day!"
>
> So she says, "Give it tae me!" *[Willie demonstrates with a sudden grabbing motion.]* An she pulls it tae a wash han basin, an gets carbolic soap an a scrubbin brush, an in wi this she goes, nae bother! But oh! The pain! I could hae seen her far enough! Worse than gettin the top o the thumb off! An after she'd cleaned it, scrubbed it, when the man had tae dae it, the surgeon, he had tae get right intae the bone tae get that bit o skin tae flap over the end. But it wasnae

> perfect, because you'll see there's a part o a nail there. He left just a wee bit o it, when he should have taken it clean away, because that wee bit could still grow. So I went back later an says, "Can you no take that oot?"
>
> "Oh," he said, "You'd have tae go through aw the system again."
>
> I say, "Och!" I wasnae goin through aw that! But you see, that corner always grows, an I have tae file it. No, it didnae stop me havin a good career, an it was partly my fault, but if I'd had a guard on the machine, I wouldnae hae done that. See what happens? Tryin tae make money one way, because we were on a bonus.

Ever resourceful, however, Willie used the thumb to demonstrate two things: Firstly, the importance of keeping to safety rules to avoid injury; and secondly, the importance of aiming for perfection in every detail, or, like the surgical repair, you'll be stuck with something that's not quite right. Dougie continues:

> You should have seen him! He used tae stand at a lathe, an you know how ladies have got nice nail files? Well, Willie would stand with a muckle big engineer's file an he'd file the bit o nail that grew on the end o the stump! We'd laugh, but this was a regular occurrence so you couldnae help bein reminded!

Ronnie smiles, as he stretches out one hand: enough said, for before we can ask how he lost the top of his finger, the 'boys' begin to discuss castings, and plans to make a commemorative plaque. John will make the pattern, and when it comes to moulding, Ronnie's the man for the job. A missing finger joint doesn't stop him doing a better job than anyone else; it might even have made him more attentive to every detail. "And by the way, did you know that Yuri Gagarin was a moulder? That's a fact," Ronnie tells us.

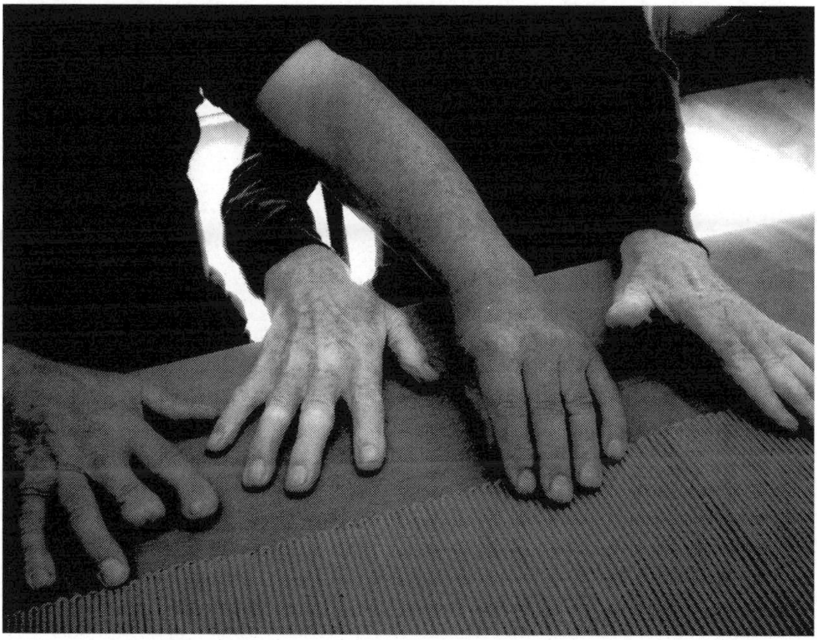

Nothing serious, but you'll no dae it again!
Losing a finger-tip or the end of a thumb turns skilled craftsman (Ronnie and Willie) into convincing teachers of Health and Safety. [G. Mazzei].

Machines and Tools of the Trade

The year at Technical College made sure that students began their apprenticeships with a good general knowledge of plant machinery, equipment, tools and instruments. From that point on, depending on the area of engineering they chose, they would become more specialised. The apprentice turners, for example, could expect to walk into the Melville-Brodie machine shop and work on machines installed by the company. Day by day they would become ever more skilled at operating them, and would also learn more about their structure and maintenance.

Everyone understood the importance of keeping machinery in top condition as the Melville-Brodie engineers were regularly called upon to rescue broken-down machinery for factories, such as linoleum works and paper mills. It went without saying, for example, that all the boys knew how a camshaft operated, not (as nowadays) from fixing cars, but because the cam was an essential part of many of their machines. As the cam has to fit the needs of the machine, the apprentices had to be familiar with every variant and function. Bob Thomson, who has long been regarded as the real expert, lit up as he remembered the journeymen who taught him:

> Cams are parts on the machine that lifts – as it revolves, it lifts, an we were workin on some job an were gettin a lot o bother because the tips o the cams was wearin. It was cast iron, an it was wearin, so they were havin trouble. So they decided what they would do: they would saw a bit oot like a T, an put a bit in, o hard steel. So they did this, they put this intae the machine. I was just a wee boy, an apprentice, an I was sent tae help the man. There was a big hurry for this because aw the bosses was fussin aboot. So we gets it on the machine, gets it ready tae start cuttin, an Willie Williamson comes up an he says, "Geordie, Geordie, is that the last ane?" An he says, "Yes, but Ah'm daein it first!"

> An one year, I was in a job workin wi copper. Noo I'd never worked wi copper before, an when I was tryin tae cut a thread in it, the tool was always breakin. So I went tae Mr. Williamson, he was the foreman, an he says, "How are you gettin on with it?"
>
> An I says, "Oh I'm havin an awfie job with it, it's breakin."
>
> He says, "Like a carrot? Well," he says tae me, "get it tae Neil."
>
> He wis the blacksmith. So what I had tae dae was take it down tae the blacksmith, an he put it in the fire an warmed it up till it was red, then dipped it in the water tae cool it. Then I put it in, an I was able tae cut it no bother. That was a wee thing that I would never have been able tae dae till he told me that. You learned aw the tricks o the trade.

Finding a solution to a problem brings great satisfactions to any job, and being able to pass it on to the next generation is one of the joys of those who take pride in their craft. Though it is more than seventy years since the blacksmith showed Bob what was needed, he recalls the day as if it was yesterday, remembering the blacksmith who taught him as well as the pleasure in being able to meet the challenge. Short anecdotes such as this turn into good stories well worth the telling, and when the teller's eyes and face light up, as in Bob's case, the story becomes all the more memorable.

Time and time again the engineers would recall in detail situations where it was not their text-book learning that stretched them or inspired further innovation, but sharing information with the likes of Bob Thomson or Willie Black. No matter where they worked, their experiences contributed to the wider pool of knowledge about every aspect of their work. Stories that began, "D'you remember yon time…" or "I mind one old guy I worked wi…" usually contained gems of information worth passing on to a fellow engineer yet, until Dougie and the 'boys' began this project, few of those stories seem to have been recorded.[16] The one that follows was recorded over twenty years ago from an old engineer who would have loved to share a pint with the boys – my father, George Bennett, who trained with a Glasgow engineering firm, A & J Mains. As it ties in so well with Bob's story, it seems worth sharing:

> When I finished my training, early Fifties, and they were doing aw those hydro schemes, a wee company in Portree needed an engineer because they got the contract for two power-stations. One was at Nostie Bridge (near Balmacarra) and one at Stor Lochs (Skye) and the stone they were using was from Lealt quarry – a type o granite, a garnet mica-type, quite hard, with a reddish tinge, an a bit o a sheen from it. And we had to truck it from the quarry – it's only a few miles from Stor Loch, but it's a long, long way from Nostie, not tae mention the ferry. So we were trying tae get the stone reasonably squared off before it left the quarry. And there was a lot o tooling tae be done, so I had six masons, two from Newcastle area, two from Aberdeenshire and two locals. An each mason was required tae carry with him his toolkit, which included two dozen chisels – special chisel-like tools, tae cut the stone – and a short-handled hammer, weighing about five pounds, with a flat face of about an inch an a half and a square head. Of course I was used tae being with a firm that had their own blacksmith and blacksmith's shop for sharpening tools – for sharpening the teeth o the back-hoes and mechanical shovels, you needed a full-time blacksmith. And my father was a blacksmith, a toolsmith, wi the Locomotive works in Glasgow

[16] The School of Scottish Studies Archive holds the recordings of my father, George Bennett (b. 1917), interviewed in Halifax, Nova Scotia, 1995. See, SSS Archive No.: SA2001.013–15. (His father, John Bennett, b. 1885, served his apprenticeship as a boilermaker in Glasgow.)

– a big manufacturing company where they made locomotive parts.

But there I was in Skye, so we went tae the local blacksmith and he didn't seem tae be having much success keeping us goin-goin-going with the properly sharpened tools. And this blacksmith in Portree was doing these daily, about a dozen for each mason, probably about fifty, sixty tools or more, but still, they would either soften at the end or, or snap off. And we were having difficulty in keeping masons going wi their tools properly sharpened.

Then my father came up on holiday so I told him o my problems, whereupon, just sittin by the fire, he asked for a small chisel – just an ordinary little chisel, an asked for a bucket o water, an a pair o tongs. An he set this chisel on the fire and he showed me how tae bring the heat up till it was just about white-hot – you could watch it, the colour would darken tae a red, and it would move up tae the point o the chisel and just as the point o the chisel was about tae lose its colour, he plunged it into this bucket o water.

Now, he didnae want tae be showing off, but my father came with me tae the blacksmith's and they tried it out, and it worked. So by this method and the chisels lasted much better, the tempering just seemed tae be right. And the blacksmith was pleased – it wasn't a case o cutting down on blacksmithing, it was keeping the men going in tools, because they'd been complaining about it.

Chisel, Melville-Brodie collection [G Mazzei].

From the outset, apprentices learned that no area of specialisation could stand alone in the context of engineering: if one part failed or broke down it would affect the whole job. Thus the apprentices soon appreciated the importance of good relationships between fellow workers. They learned to move with ease from one department to another, some working on big equipment installed in the plant (such as the turners and fitters) and others, such as the patternmakers, with smaller tools or instruments. Having chosen to be a patternmaker, John Greig recalled what it was like as a new apprentice:

> The patternmakers had tae buy an awful lot o tools compared tae the other trades but they got a tool allowance, which they were expected tae spend on their tools, replacin tools an buyin tools in the first place. When you began the apprenticeship, if you were lucky you had a loan or the use o a tool belongin tae the company or tae another foreman. Without that you couldn't do your job.

As tools and instruments were of prime importance, junior patternmakers would take advice on buying instruments to be proud of, and tools to last a lifetime. Apprentice moulders also had to have a variety of tools, though, as Ronnie explained, the last thing they'd want would be a brand new set. "Hopeless! You'd be ready to retire before they got worn down to the way you wanted them." Thus began Ronnie's introduction to a few tools of his trade[17]:

> Moulders' tools werenae o use tae anybody else, an they were often home-made, or maist o them. There was a knack tae acquirin them – when one o the journeymen was comin up for retirement, maybe a year before, you'd start playin up tae him, helpin him

[17] These, along with other moulding tools, are listed by John F. Buchanan in the glossary of over 1,000 foundry terms compiled for his book, *Foundry Nomenclature: the Moulder's Pocket Dictionary*, (London & New York, 1903.)

out, like, "Can I dae that fir ye?" You'd be hopin that he'd leave you some o his tools, for new tools were more or less hopeless, havin tae be broken in. Likes, I've a *cleaner* oot there, you know, an if you'd seen the size o it when it was new, now it's worn an it's perfect now for doin the tricky stuff an that. An the moulder's name is on it, Wull Kay, he was a great moulder.

Well, the main tool was a wee trowel, but we caw that a 'troon'.[18] You had tae have several sizes for different jobs – but there was only one maker o foundry tools that I remember – it was T. Monk. An they made the best o quality, wi a wee monk stamped on them, an that first troon would dae you aw your life. An you had a *finishin troon,* which had started off as a normal troon, an it would be worn down tae a nice size for doin finishin work. An then there was *cleaners,* which were long-bladed tools, like a knife, maybe 9 inches long, an turned up at right angles an flattened – that would scoop bits o the sand out, for the moulds were aw sand. Then you had *clubs* – a club had a cleaner blade an the foot was mair substantial: it had edges on it, an you used that for when the mould was finished. You used tae dust it with plumbago, from a bag, which was more or less graphite – graphite an lead. An then you had tae have *sleekers,* so when you sleeked it, you'd dust it an take your tools over it an it would come up a nice sheen. But if you overdone it, you would draw the dampness from the sand tae the surface which you didnae want, in fact some places they just brushed it on, an they never bothered sleekin it. There was a range o tools for that – you had *swans necks* an *deuk's nebs* an *fillets.* They were usually made o brass, an the *fillets* were aw different sizes dependin on the curvature o the

[18] There are alternative spellings of the word. The *Dictionary of the Older Scottish Tongue* cites 'truan' and 'trooan' as alternatives, while the on-line Scots Dictionary gives 'trouen'.

mould. An then *flange sleekers*. An you had a *joint-sleeker*, that was the first one you used – a simple mould was in two halves, so when you separated the mouldin boxes an took the pattern oot, often the edges could be broken round about, so they had tae patched up. An you had a right-angled joint-sleeker, so that you took that along. Actually if you'd seen a finished mould, especially if Bert Lindsay at Melville-Brodie's had worked on it, he was the champion at finishin moulds! They were aw like silver, sittin there, an your *flange sleeker* went roond the edge an that left an even edge, the same bridth aw round the mould. An then we had a *tricky*, that's like a double-sided sleeker, an there was the *wee tricky*.

The foundry used tae use flour for markin things, an it was the sweepins fae the flour-mill we used tae get, an this was an attraction for the mice an rats. Often a job was left open, tae let air aboot it, because if you closed it, condensation could occur in the mould, an molten metal an dampness or water didnae mix. So we'd see wee footprints aroun aboot the mould – mice or bigger, even rats. So once, when we were makin the big sole-plates for the paper-makin machinery, we had a wee encounter wi a moose! If you'd cast it, an there was a moose or a rat inside it, if that landed up on a bit that was machined, it'd leave a big hole, never mind aboot the poor moose or rat. So we decided tae dismantle this mould, tae see if we could find it, an we were taken oot the cores, which form the internal part o the mould, takin them oot one by one. An everybody was roond the mould wi sticks tae clobber this culprit! But the last core was lifted oot, an still no moose, an here it was, hingin on tae the underside o this core! An so we put it doon, an it ran away – we didnae get it!

You need tae have a steady hand tae be a moulder, an steady feet, because you had tae watch where you

> were standin in the foundry, because the floor could be very uneven. But I still have a wee foundry in my garage, an what I dae there is fun! Like, last week I was makin an engine part for a First World War aeroplane – this being the hundredth anniversary, the museum was doin one up, so I made a 4-arm spider-clamp – that's the bit for holding the cylinder head. I'm daein up my 1936 Rudge motorbike – I make reproduction parts for old motor bikes, because you cannae buy them, but I can dae that in my wee foundry, an I still have some tools oot there.

As he laid them out one by one, Ronnie stepped back to admire them, quietly reciting a verse composed by a fellow-foundry worker, who came from Falkirk:

> While cleanin my tools the other day,
> Back through the years I took my way,
> Jist bits o iron, steel an brass,
> The average man would kick an pass,
> But tae me, they are my kith an kin,
> Wi foondrie saund they've worn thin.
>
> **[Russell, Falkirk]**

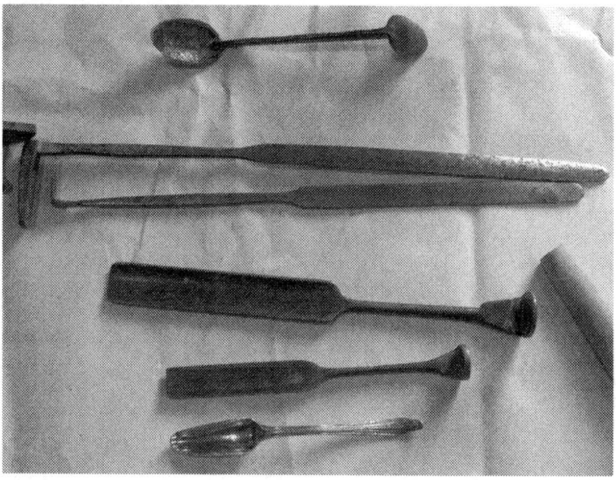

Some of Ronnie's foundry tools, from top to bottom: spoon sleeker; club; cleaner; tricky; wee tricky; spoon sleeker.

Ronnie in his 'wee foondry' and some of his tools, 2014.

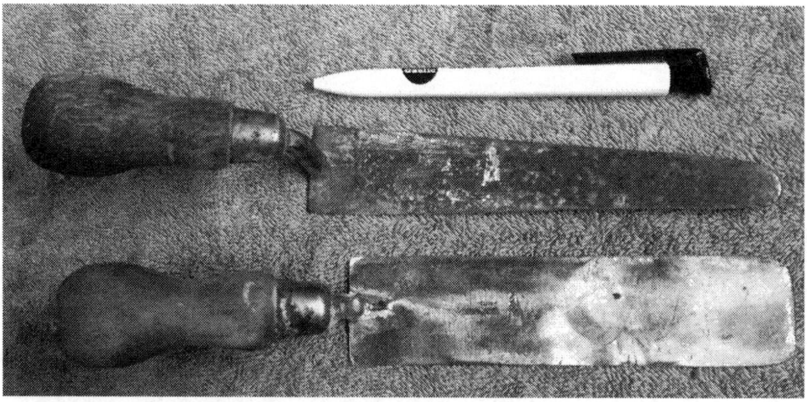

A finishin troon an wan that's square, for takin aw the wear an tear!

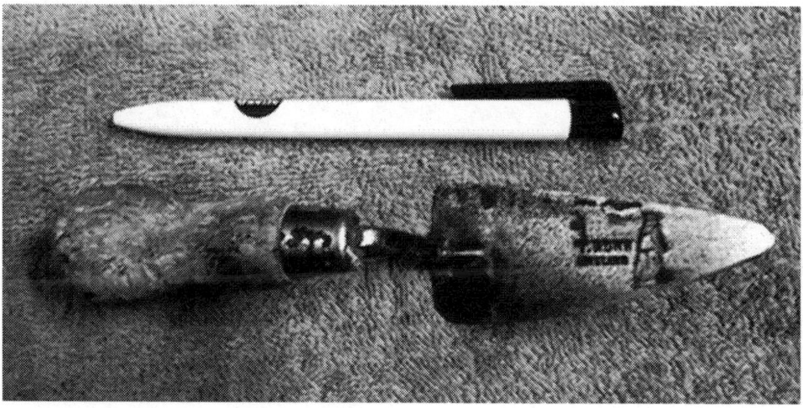

The wee troon, stamped with the Monk.

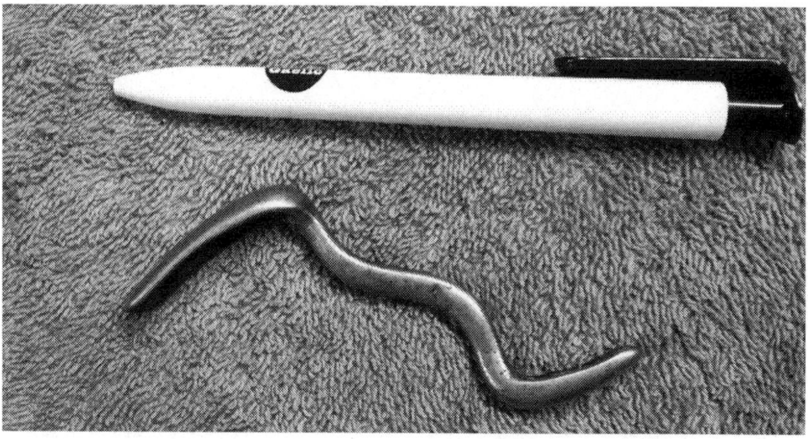

The deuk's neb. Hand-made of brass, the date stamped on it is 1884.

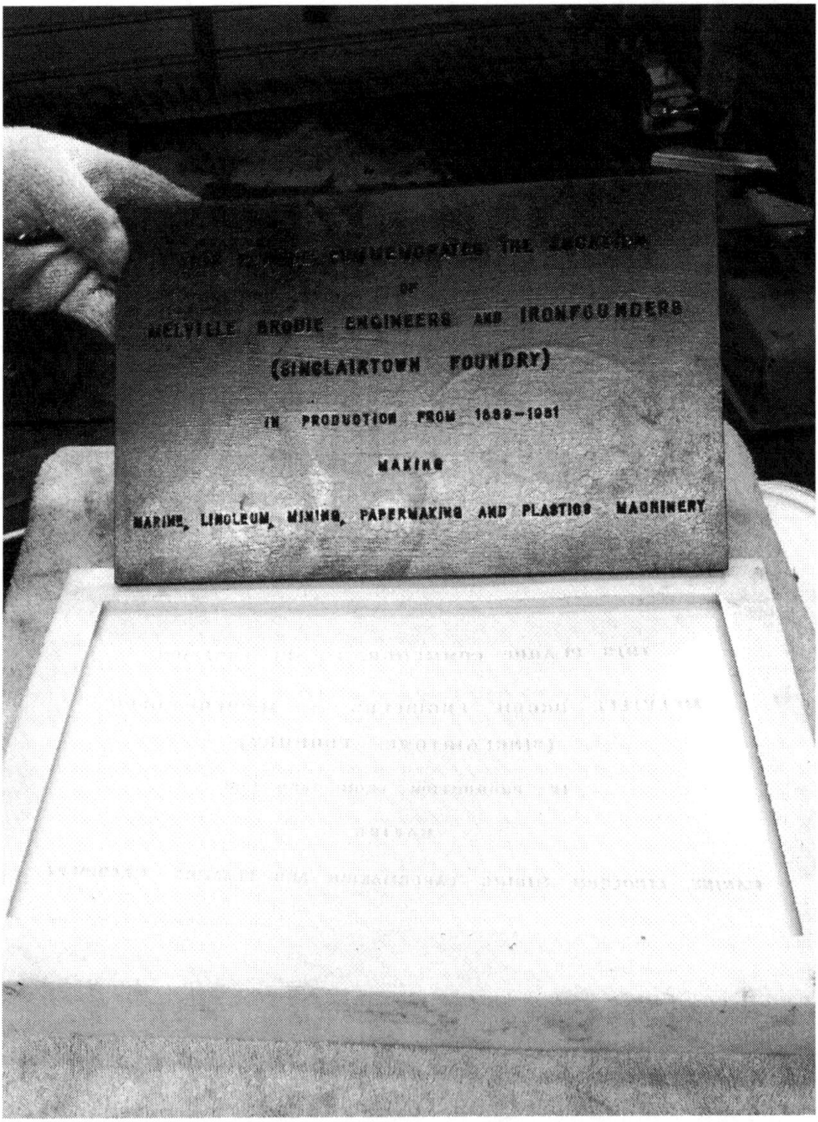

The pattern for this plaque was made by John Greig and cast by Ronnie Fleming. It commemorates the location of Melville-Brodie Engineering Co., in Kirkcaldy, and was unveiled on 14 May 2014.

MACHINES:

Grace's Guide to British Industrial History includes machines designed and built by Melville-Brodie Engineering Company, <www.gracesguide.co.uk>.

Six-Roll Mill Melville-Brodie.

Three-roll linoleum mixer. Melville-Brodie.

Linoleum Printing Machine for 18 Inch blocks. Melville-Brodie.

MACHINES: Mrs June Shanks photo collection

Five-Roll linoleum mixer. [JS].

Melville-Brodie linoleum mixer. [JS].

Melville-Brodie compressor, 1920. [JS].

Melville-Brodie linoleum mixers. [JS].

An industrial pump, designed and made to order by Melville-Brodie . [JS].

Melville-Brodie Pump machine. [JS].

Melville-Brodie cement mixer. [JS].

Sport, Leisure and Social Life

In every organisation the level of morale can make or break relationships at work. When Robert Burt Brodie and William Kilgour formed Melville-Brodie Engineering Company in 1918, they were not only building on a reputation for top-class engineering but also for good work ethics. Having come up through the ranks himself, when Brodie became sole owner in 1921 he stuck to these principles. Bob Thomson remembers: "When I first started we had a football team, and Mr. Brodie had supplied aw the gear, strips, the ball and boots an everything. An the other thing, they had a summer drive, which Mr. Brodie paid for." Lads who didn't have two pennies to rub together, far less buy a football-strip, appreciated the generosity and good spirit which benefited everyone. But, as Bob wistfully recalled, "you'll aye find someone to spoil it for everybody else."

Then there was a time some o them had misused it, maybe no doin what they were supposed to, so gradually the organised football went into disuse. An then on one o the summer outins, some o them overdid it wi the drink, an they were fightin, an so it aw got stopped.

The disappointment did not last, however, as the ban was later lifted when it was clear that Mr. Brodie had made his point. Summer outings were reinstated and the firm supported other social events that gave free reign to the creative, imaginative and talented workforce. Boilersuits and dungarees aside, these lads proved they could 'clean up good' and put on a great show. As for sports activities, football and cycling needed little organising as they were already a way of life for most.

For annual outings, the firm would hire buses to take the entire workforce to a chosen destination, generally on the west coast. As very few people had cars until the 1970s, a day's excursion was a real treat. For many of the boys, their first Melville-Brodie outing was also the first time they had travelled from the east coast of Scotland to the west. Those who so wished could also invite family members, and for the married men with children the 'works day out' was a special treat. Willie played a major role in organising it, and as Dougie remembered, he'd laughingly tell the apprentices, "We'll put aw you toe-rags on the one bus," and as they went aboard, would remind them all to be back at the bus at the appointed time. One year it was Oban, and another it was Ayr or Helensburgh with a trip 'doon the watter' on the paddle steamer, 'The PS Waverley'. As the whole workforce travelled together, families got to know each other, and it was one day when apprentices were not constantly under the watchful eye of journeymen or bosses. (They knew, however, about the expectation of 'responsible behaviour' and they were not about to repeat history.) The main aim was to pack as much fun as possible into the day's freedom, to get to know folk better, share a picnic or a meal, explore new places or find out about local landmarks, 'talent' or curiosities. The teenagers' inspection tour of MacNab's Folly in Oban, for example, had been well worth the brisk walk to the summit, though more recently the same 'brae' seems to have turned into a long, steep climb. Full of energy, the young apprentices could walk for miles, visit the local chippie, share wild ideas over a pint or chat up the local girls. When it was time to get back on the bus, the boys all turned up, and if senior management were impressed at their time-keeping, Dougie gave away the game:

> We'd have a quiet word wi the driver, an we'd ask him tae be sure and get back tae Kirkcaldy tae catch a last pint! In those days, closin time was half-past nine until you reached the Forth at Kincardine, then in Fife it was 10 p.m. So you had tae be back at the bus bang on time! And if the worst came tae the worst, and it didnae look like we'd be in Kirkcaldy in time, say we were held up in traffic, we'd ask the bus driver tae stop in Kincardine for a toilet break – and o course we were all straight intae the nearest pub!

Most industrial towns in Scotland have an established tradition of an annual 'trades holiday' when workplaces close for two weeks.

It was a welcome holiday and often a time to visit relatives. Kirkcaldy, as John explained, was in line with the rest of the Fifeshire:

> Fife Trades were normally the fortnight nearest to the 14th – that keeps it to second week o July. Edinburgh overlapped with Fife, the same fortnight, but Dundee had a separate fortnight, an so did Glasgow, an they call it the 'Glasgow Fair' – the whole place closed down.

On a Saturday during that fortnight, Kirkcaldy holds its annual Pageant, which is a community event in every sense. It has a long history reflecting a strong spirit of goodwill, and in bringing everybody together it raises funds for charities and those in need. Writing for the *Statistical Account* in 1845, the Rev. Alexander noted that Kirkcaldy's first charity was formed in 1591, and was set up to aid disabled mariners as well as widows and orphans.

From the time Melville-Brodie Engineering Company was founded, the firm had been committed to making a major contribution to the good of community. Dougie and his fellow apprentices were also aware of the background:

When the company first started, we have tae remember that hospitals an hospices had tae be kept up by local donations o money. There was no such thing as National Health Service – that didnae begin till the late Forties. So, Melville-Brodie's played no small part in raisin money, an on Pageant Days it was a chance for the entire workforce tae get involved. An you should have seen some o the lengths they went to, aw these engineers an apprentices!

When Bob Thomson joined the firm in the mid-Thirties, he sensed that the strong connection community concerns had a lot to do with Robert Burt Brodie's involvement in the Kirkcaldy Council. When he was first elected in 1915, Brodie was one of the partners in Melville-Henderson's. Serving on several key committees he was known for his commitment to making a difference, so was re-elected in 1920. By that time he had become co-director of Melville-Brodie Engineering Company.

When it came to the annual Pageant Day, Mr. Brodie could scarcely have been more supportive, considering the time and expense that went into making the 'weird and wonderful' Melville-Brodie creations. Looking at Pageant Day photos, Dougie explained that they would sometimes choose themes that were current news, such as some new invention or contraption and they would have great fun putting it together for the day. If the scale of radio theme seems disproportionate to a generation that expects audio-technology to be at everybody's fingertips, it is worth remembering that most homes in Scotland did not have a radio till the Second World War. There was no such thing as a small radio, and even in the 1950s, the 'wireless' (as it was called), usually sat on a sturdy shelf and was powered by a huge, heavy accumulator.[19] As every engineer knows, keeping abreast of technology is a way of life. New inventions are part of everyday conversation, and so, when the wireless was 'hot news', that was the theme chosen by the Melville-Brodie boys. Exaggerated as it now may seem, a visit to a museum of technology will confirm that the predecessors of modern computers were so massive that some occupied an entire room. Though primarily designed to amuse and satirise technology, the scale of Melville-Brodie's radio construction nevertheless reflects the experimentation of the era.

Original ideas came from all departments and every skill could be mustered to create something that would be out of the question for unskilled groups. On the day, the team would take its place in a huge parade made up of all ages from every kind of occupation (or none), all representing the best of Kirkcaldy. Folk hoped for fine weather so the whole town could turn out. John Greig outlined a typical parade:

> It was always on the weekend an there was a big pageant that went through the town, all for the

[19] As a child, I remember one time when my father disconnected the battery to take it to a garage to be re-charged, he let me try to lift it but it was too heavy!

> purpose o raisin money for the hospitals. It always came from the ice rink in Kirkcaldy, then it used tae come doon Rosslyn Street, right doon tae where the hospital was – what we called the General Hospital. Then from there, doon the path an right along the High Street. An the Fire Brigade would be takin part in the pageant, with a fire-truck, an the fireman used tae have the long poles, an on the end o the pole was like an enormous kirk-collection bag. An you didnae escape, even if you were up in a high window, say, lookin doon watchin it, a fireman could always reach you! An you got a bag shoved in yer face tae get the pennies oot an get them in the bag. An then down at Ravenscraig Park, you could see them all. But sometimes we went tae Bevvie Park.

As there were some talented entertainers among the workforce, they too were featured on Pageant Day. Dougie remembered some of the stalwarts who 'did a turn':

> They had various characters, for example, one guy that I remember, Albert Kydd, he was a fitter, an he was a very, very good amateur illusionist. An there was another guy who imitated Sir Harry Lauder, complete with his crooked stick.
>
> For Pageant Day, everyone would pitch in, an some o the apprentices used tae dress up tae collect money. I got dressed up for one o the pageants, an one year we made this box, like a soap-powder box. Mind, they used tae get soap powders called 'Omo'? Well, the name on mine was 'Oma'. An they made it up so it slipped over my head, an my head was aw painted as well, an me in this box. An there I was, walkin doon the road wi ma hand oot the box, wi ma collection thingy. An the smart ones that didnae fancy gettin aw dolled up, what they'd dae was tae sit on the lorry an collect the pennies. Folk would fling them onto the

> lorry an the boys on the float collected them cos they didnae want tae dress up, walkin aroun bein made a bloody fool o! But it was full o fun.

Kirkcaldy still has its Pageant Days, and entertaining as it is to watch the parade, it's even more enjoyable to be part of it.[20]

The Melville-Brodie float constructed around Mr. Brodies's Buick. The team are all set to go, and so is their driver, Robert Burt Brodie.

---

[20] The Scottish Screen Archive has a black and white film of the 1952 pageant, which shows many of the aspects described here, including the long-handled collecting bags, floats, street entertainers, and competitions for children (such as the biggest and smallest dog contest). Though there is no sound-track, the film captures the atmosphere of the town as well as hospital visits. See: <ssa.nls.uk/film/1648>.

The works outing: Left to right: Bill Simpson, Arch McGilvray, Dougie Reid, John Whiltehill, Don Barclay, Dave Nicol, Will Brown, Ernie Sharp, Derek White, Charles Brewster, 1960. [MM]

Left to right: Arch McGilvary, John Whitehill, Don Barclay, Dave Nicol, Will Brown, Ernie Sharp, Derek White, Charles Brewster and Dougie Reid, 1960. [MM]

Left to right: Matthew Morrison, Dougie Reid and Bill Simpson.1960. [MM]

There were occasional staff events and always time for a pint on the way home…. Left to right: Dougie Reid, Chick McCann, Charles Brewster and Dick Shan. [MM]

Calling all radio hams! Melville-Brodie engineers on Kirkcaldy Pageant Day (1930s), Mr. Brodie even lent his car!

Unity is Strength

From the drawing office to the foundry, no matter the craft, there was an infectious sense of pride. It went without saying, "If a job's worth doing, it's worth doing well – that's with you aw your life." And, as Dougie added:

> This was also a union thing – Willie was a shop steward for years, an he wouldnae stand any nonsense. An he would ken if you'd made a mistake an before you went into a meetin, he'd say, now Dougie, did you dae it right? An as long as he went through that door with you into the boss, he knew he was standin next tae someone who was honest and integrity sound.

If an apprentice stayed the course he could look forward to becoming a time-served journeyman with papers to prove that he had served his time with Melville-Brodie Engineering Company. As Dougie said, "You'd have two things: your apprenticeship papers and your union card, both pinned together. And when you got that, with Melville-Brodie's name on the top, you could go anywhere in the world to work for any engineering company."

Being members of the Engineering Federation of Employers (the organisation providing guidance on employment law, employee relations, health and safety, etc.), Melville-Brodie Engineering Company paid their apprentices at the rate set at national level. They continually advised all apprentices to join a union, and not to wait (as in some companies) until they had become time-served journeymen. As Ronnie explained:

> Aw the trades had their own union – we were the Amalgamated Union of Foundry Workers. We used tae get a monthly journal tellin us where aw the work was, which foundry was busy, an which foundry was in use. Dougie's membership is the

> Amalgamated Engineering Union, an John's the United Patternmakers Association, the UPA.[21]

The apprentices were all part of a long tradition that had produced some of Scotland's foremost engineers. Tradition does not stand still, however, as it can only serve its purpose when willing to adapt and progress. This does not imply change for the sake of change, however, but an understanding of what works best. While there are advantages to keeping a Victorian crane, (it did the job better than any other), there are disadvantages in binding apprentices to terms and conditions from a former era.

For several years, apprentices all over the country had asked their unions to review their pay-scale, particularly the percentage of the adult rate, which had become so outdated it was becoming untenable. Trade union meetings, conferences, negotiations and discussions came and went, but with no resolution of this issue. As union members, all the apprentices knew their motto, 'unity is strength', so in 1960, some of them decided to put it to the test.

[21] An archive of records is housed at the University of Warwick Library, Coventry CV4 7AL. For access, email: <archives@warwick.ac.uk>.

The National Apprentices' Strike

Looking back to the episode that was to mark a milestone in British labour history, Dougie began:

> At Melville-Brodie's we were a strong union shop, as we said, Willie Black was our shop steward an management relationships were very good. But, as a member o the Employers' Federation, our bosses just had tae follow national engineerin wage rates an conditions, so they were well within the law. However, on a national scale, apprentices had a genuine crib, which was that the percentages were far too low. For example, a five-year apprentice, in his improving year, only received 62.5 percent o a craftsman's wage.[22] There were plenty o arithmetical experts among them capable o calculatin the amount they were undervalued – an it was considerable. They stated their case, but the unions were takin forever tae sort it out. So there was a strike, a national situation affectin all o us. I was on the committee, an so a dozen o us, or so, fae Melville-Brodie's, we were aw set tae go tae wherever the demonstration was takin place. There was a fund set aside for bus or train fares, whatever was best.

Among the Trades Union Executive members whose sympathies lay with the apprentices was solicitor, political activist and writer Angela Tuckett (1906–1994). In her book, *The Blacksmiths' History: What Smithy Workers Gave Trade Unionism,* Tuckett summed up what happened in a chapter entitled "The Apprentices Make History":

> One of the most energetic and lively actions, which rapidly took on a national character, was a remarkable

[22] The 'improving year' is the fifth and final year.

> movement amongst the shipbuilding and engineering apprentices... The claim for improved youth rates had first been submitted as long ago as 1953. ... The latest claim for an all-round increase in their percentage of the journeyman's rate had been two and a half years in negotiations without result. It was renewed in April, 1959 ...But many months passed with no sign of a meeting until exasperated Clydeside apprentices held a one-day token strike on February 24, 1960, in protest against the delay. Then the employers agreed to meet the Confederation on April 20th... a year and eleven days after the request was first made. As a demonstration of their support for the claim ... apprentices from all over Scotland downed tools that day. Next morning some of the employers suspended those who had taken part: that set the heather alight. Journeymen at Singer's in Clydebank and in six shipyards ... stopped work in protest... By May Day some 36,000 apprentices were out in Scotland ... Soon it spread throughout England, from Merseyside, Manchester and Lancashire ... Belfast ... More and more demonstrations in lively style went on through the first two weeks of May until the employers agreed to consider the claim and give an answer within the month.

With over 60,000 apprentices on the picket lines, including the Melville-Brodie boys, the strike was front-page news. Day after day, the *Glasgow Herald,* for example, had headlines such as 'Boy Strikers Told to Return: Union Advice on the Eve of Pay Talks', with a controversial article in the adjacent column, 'Two Rebuffs for Strike Committee: Parents Support Employers' (3rd May, 1960). Dougie recalled the strategy for organising demonstrations, with apprentices the length and breadth of the country keeping in touch with each other via a network of communication that no officials had anticipated:

> There was no internet then, mind! But we had folk on bicycles, motor-bikes, auld bangers, even runners, an we were determined we'd aw be there, wherever an whenever the apprentice committee decided. We'd be there, ready tae demonstrate, tae march, tae sing, an shout our slogan! "Two pound twelve an six!" That was what we shouted! It was all over the papers, but an a lot o them didnae dae us any good the way they reported.

Singing as a means of protest has an extensive history – even Charles Dickens mentions it[23] – but, as social historian Roy Palmer notes, factory owners have long recognised the power of singing protest songs, and were even known to take legal action to stop it.[24] During the 1961 strike, the apprentices were aware that, while very few of them would be given an opportunity to speak on any public platform, singing or chanting their message was the only way to be heard. On May 11th a so-called 'unofficial march' through Glasgow, accompanied by youthful singing and shouting attracted police and a headline of '44 Young Strikers Arrested' (12th May) though there was no cause to detain the boys. The following day, May 13th, the headline read, 'Apprentices May End Strike: Unions Order Return to Work to Help Negotiations' and the day after, (May 14th) the announcement was: 'Apprentices May Decide Today: Unions Call for Return to Work".

Having reviewed the national media coverage of the time, social historian Sandy Hobbs observed that newspaper reports seemed to stir up the entire country:

> From many quarters, employers, union officials and the press, came accusations of communist dominance,

---

[23] Charles Dickens, *In Household Words,* (1853), p. 347. Quoted by Roy Palmer (1988), p. 18.

[24] Roy Palmer gives an example from mill-workers demonstrating in Preston in 1853, when "the magistrates had given orders to the policemen to prevent the turn-outs [demonstrators] from singing in the streets." See, Roy Palmer, *The Sound of History: Songs and Social Comment,* (1988), p. 19, as well as his discussion on the use of song in recent labour disputes, pp. 84–109.

> intimidation and general irresponsibility on the part of what they liked to call the 'Boy Strikers'.[25]

Despite condescending insinuations and the tension surrounding the strike, even the union officials did not anticipate the determination of the apprentices or the support they had from their journeymen. Apprentices at Melville-Brodies's were among them, as Dougie recalled:

> This was a national strike – the main full-time union officials in London told us tae get back tae work an we aw refused. The apprentices had worked oot that the average amount we were undervalued was calculated tae be £2-12s-6d[26] a week, so that became the slogan, loudly voiced at every meetin. "Two pound twelve an six!" That was what we shouted!

If apprentices sensed that national newspapers paid scant attention to what the apprentices said, sang, or shouted, there may have been more confidence elsewhere, particularly in the world of folk music. Folksong clubs, which had been springing up all over Britain since the mid-1950s, traditionally reflect an identity with working class people, and generally lend moral, political and financial support where needed. Within the world of folk music, there was a keen understanding that this was a national strike, and singers and song-makers adapted old songs, made new, and sang in support of the striking apprentices. The unique power in thousands of voices singing together resonates with the union motto, 'Unity is strength'. At every demonstration the apprentices chanted and sang the length and breadth of the country, sticking stuck to their guns, as Dougie recalled:

---

[25] Sandy Hobbs is an Honorary Research Fellow at the West of Scotland University. His books in include *Child Labour: A World History Companion*, 1999. This comment is quoted from his on-line article, 'Clyde Apprentices' Strikes', accessed via <citystrolls.com/a-real-peoples-history/sandy-hobbs/>.

[26] Today, £2.63.

> The trade union officials told us tae get back tae work; the government told us tae get back tae work; the Employers Federation was tellin us tae get back tae work. But the craftsmen in aw the factories were one hundred percent behind us, an so were a lot o the employers, but the employers daren't pay anythin against their federation. an it took a tremendous effort but eventually it succeeded. An we got the percentages altered – nothin like we were lookin for, but it made the point. an in my opinion, it helped tae gel the current crew – it got people interested, because we became quite involved. It was a real milestone for all o us.

The apprentices made history in June when they organised a mass-lobby in South Wales at the annual conference of the Confederation of unions. Angela Tuckett reported that, "They impressed everyone by their spirit, discipline and maturity," and when they were allowed into conference, "Standing Orders were suspended to allow delegates to hear their spokesman, Donald McLaren, the Secretary of the Clyde Apprentices Committee." In conclusion, she noted, the chair of the conference, Frank Foulkes, was of the opinion that:

> The trade unions to which they belong should be proud of them... [Union officials had seen for themselves that Britain's future craftsmen] displayed organising ability, self-discipline, enterprise, good behaviour and good manners. In their demonstrations and deputations they proved that they possessed all the essential qualifications for successful agitation and negotiations together with a sense of humour and tolerance.[27]

Although the pay settlement that followed gave them considerably less than they had aimed for, as Sandy Hobbs put

[27] Tuckett, p. 355.

it, the "apprentices had shown their industrial power and drawn attention to the 'Cheap Labour Racket'." During the strike, Ronnie recalled, "the apprentices got strike pay for three weeks runnin and we got it back-dated. I mind gettin the wheels for my bike!" Not all firms had treated their workers so well, however, as McLaren later revealed that some, outwith the Employers Federation, had tried to force boys back to work by sending intimidating letters to parents, threatening harsh discipline for apprentices who did not comply. Finally, and not before time, some attention was given to the need for revision of the ancient terms of an indentureship, which, in the past, could allow for exploitation and misused power.

When the strike was over, apprentices all over the country emerged with a much higher level of confidence than ever before. Later that year, Donald McLaren summed up his experience for an article in the *Labour Monthly*:

> Boys who had never uttered more than three or four consecutive sentences became budding public speakers, holding forth to thousands of apprentices, arguing a direct, forceful and sincere case. They travelled all over Britain, addressing meetings. They appeared on TV and organized mass lobbies of trade union conferences....The organizational ability of some of my fellow apprentices was a real surprise. Lads I had known for months, even years, amazed me by the business-like way in which they carried through the job of organizing the strike. The Finance Committee handling hundreds of pounds with the ease of Wall Street bankers. The Propaganda Committee storming Clydeside with their leaflets, whitewashing teams and factory-gate meetings, that would have put the Labour Party elections boys to shame.... One thing certainly occurred to me: if most of my companions were half as good at their trade as they were at fighting the bosses, then they deserved double the money that we were asking for!

> .... The strike is over and we have been awarded increases ranging from 4s. at fifteen to 16s. at twenty years.[28] Certainly this falls a long way short of what we were fighting for, an average of £2. 12s. 6d. per week; but, of one thing we are all convinced and that is, had it not been for our determined strike action, we would not have received a penny, far less 16s.[29]

Over forty years on, Sandy Hobbs reflected on the importance of the apprentice-led strike. Describing it as "one of the biggest strikes of the decade", involving over 60,000 workers and a loss of 347,000 man-days, he concluded: "There have been no more apprentice strikes of that size, and we can expect no more. Heavy engineering has declined, and with it both apprenticeships and the industrial strength of apprentices."[30]

More than a decade later, the Amalgamated Union of Engineering Workers made a film about the Union (renamed in 1970) and the Union's contribution to International Women's Year (1975). The soundtrack consisted of two songs: 'We are the Engineers' composed and sung by Ewan MacColl, and 'I Wanna be an Engineer' by Peggy Seeger. The AUEW also produced a 7-inch EP record (45rpm), with a bright red sleeve, entitled "Amalgamated Union of Engineering Workers: Unity is Strength". Dougie was fortunate to be able to obtain the disc when it was released, and he treasures his copy, which is now a collector's item.

In a world where people seldom recognise the massive contribution engineers make to everyday life – industry, transport, agriculture and civilization – Ewan MacColl's song, 'We Are the Engineers' is a lasting reminder of the remarkable skills of all the workers:

---

[28] In today's currency, 20p for fifteen-year-olds and 80p for twenty- year-olds. Of prime importance, however, was that the percentage of a craftsman's wage had been amended.

[29] Donald McLaren, *Labour Monthly*, Oct. 1960, reprinted by Angela Tuckett (1974), pp. 398-99.

[30] S. Hobbs, "Clyde Apprentices' Strikes" online blog in City Strolls, <citystrolls.com/a-real-peoples-history/sandy-hobbs/>

WE ARE THE ENGINEERS!

'Two Joined Hands' was our device
when our banner first unfurled,
Hands that knew the feel of tools
and helped to build a world.
Two hands became a million hands
and fashioned down the years
The machines that make the world go round,
The ships and planes and the diesel trains,
The weaving frames and the building cranes,
We are the engineers!

We tamed the fire and harnessed metals,
learned a thousand skills;
Our hands have made the tools men use
in factories, mines and mills.
Ours the hands that throw the switch
that puts the world in gear,
That make the ploughs that turn the soil,
And the ships and planes and the diesel trains,
The weaving frames and the building cranes,
We are the engineers!

Those who came before us walked a dark and lonely road:
Hunger, hurt and poverty, they bore a heavy load.
Police and spies at every turn, a world of doubt and fear ...
But they fought the cruel laws and when
They lost they rose to fight again,
For the right to work and live like men,
They were the engineers!

We've stamped our feet in the morning queues,
known unemployment's toll,
Known hands go soft in idleness,
the slow death on the dole.
The rusty lathe and the silent factory

mark the hungry years,
And the grass growing green on the shipyard floor,
And the endless beat of marching feet
And men demanding the right to eat
And work as engineers!

Our skills were used to fight a war, September '39,
To rid the world of fascism our workers did combine.
Men and women side by side
worked through the angry years,
And we built the tools of victory,
The bombs and guns and the armoured trains,
The tanks and ships and the fighting planes,
We are the engineers!

Two hands joined in unity have built this world of ours;
And they have built our union, too,
a tool of workers' power:
A mighty, multi-purpose tool
that cuts and bores and shears,
Combining skills of those who build
The ships and planes and the diesel trains,
The weaving frames and the building cranes,
We are the engineers!

And we, the youngest engineers,
we march to claim our rights;
We have learned that nothing's ever
won without a fight.
Every battle fought and won
reveals a new frontier,
And a world to be won by those who build
The ships and planes and the diesel trains,
The weaving frames and the building cranes,
We are the engineers![31]

---

[31] Reproduced by kind permission of Ewan MacColl Ltd. Special thanks to Peggy Seeger for her generous support.

After the strike ended, the apprentices were glad to go back to work to continue their training and become fully-qualified journeymen. With five years under their belts, the young men already knew the range of jobs they may be required to do, many at short notice. In terms of designing, manufacturing and maintaining machinery or equipment, John Greig summed up their capabilities: "Melville-Brodie engineers could turn a hand to anything – a camera casing, or an engine block, dough mixers for catering on big ships, or part of the Forth Bridge – it didnae matter."

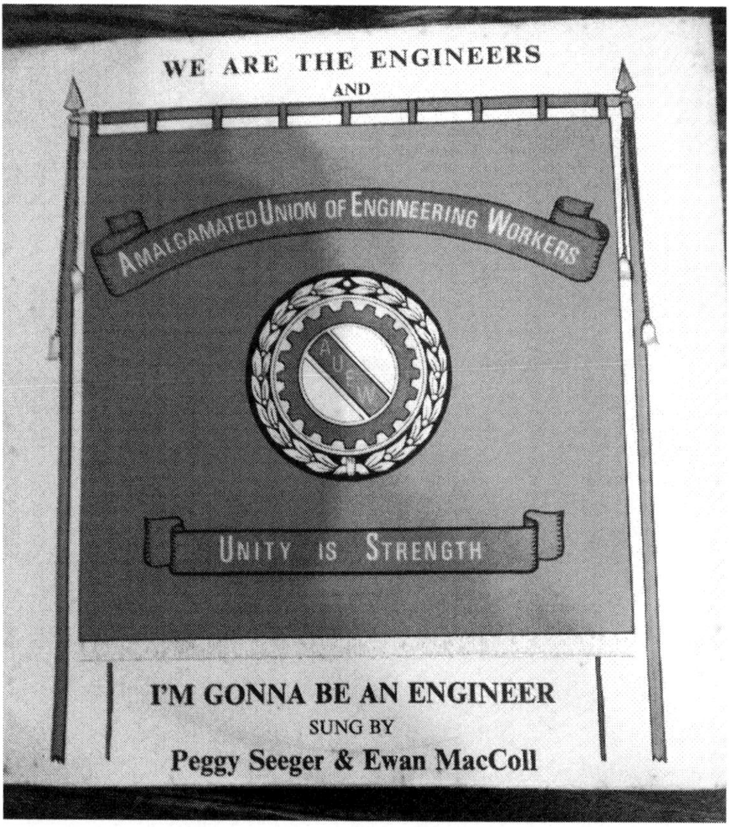

The 7-inch EP (45 rpm) record produced by the Amalgamated Union of Engineering Workers (AUEW).

Another Eventful Year

In 1961, having reached the age of 66, Jock Brodie decided to step down as Company Director, hopefully to have a longer retirement than his father had enjoyed. Though Jock had been boss since his father retired, he was not the sole owner, however, as Robert Burt Brodie had left the firm in trust to the family. After decades of supplying and fitting equipment for coal companies, linoleum factories, glass and bottleworks, shipyards, dyeworks, and mills producing cotton, wool, silk and paper, Melville-Brodie Engineering Company enjoyed a first class reputation. Their reliability proved an attractive proposition to a firm in Leith that specialised in paper-making machinery, James Bertram and Sons,[32] and so, in 1961 Melville-Brodie's changed hands. Though bought out by Bertrams, the company's name in Kirkcaldy remained the same, but the letterhead and logo would, from then on, represent the new owners.

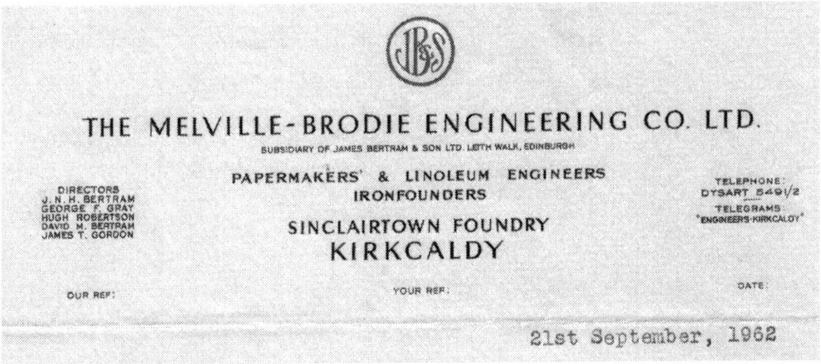
THE MELVILLE-BRODIE ENGINEERING CO. LTD.
SUBSIDIARY OF JAMES BERTRAM & SON LTD. LEITH WALK, EDINBURGH
PAPERMAKERS' & LINOLEUM ENGINEERS
IRONFOUNDERS
SINCLAIRTOWN FOUNDRY
KIRKCALDY

DIRECTORS
J. N. H. BERTRAM
GEORGE F. GRAY
HUGH ROBERTSON
DAVID M. BERTRAM
JAMES T. GORDON

TELEPHONE:
DYSART 5491/2
TELEGRAMS:
"ENGINEERS KIRKCALDY"

OUR REF: YOUR REF: DATE:

21st September, 1962

The Managing Director was David Bertram, who was based in Leith, and apart from the appointment of a new factory manager, Mr. James Gordon, the change-over did not initially affect the Kirkcaldy workforce. Dougie recalled that:

---

32 This company should not be confused with another company owned by brothers of the same family, Bertram's of Edinburgh, which was on Sciennes Road. Though owned and operated brothers, and descended from several generations of Bertrams who developed paper-making machinery, the Leith company was a separate entity.

> We got on fine ... they were good tae work for. There were some o the ways a wee bit different, but you'd expect that. They were good people... Willie and I visited David Bertram in Edinburgh not that long ago, after we'd aw retired, an when we got there he was so pleased tae see Willie especially. He poured Willie a dram... Willie was the main one he would deal with in Kirkcaldy and they got on really well.

The production of machinery continued, and so did the apprenticeship scheme, though the main headquarters were in Leith. In an interview with James Bertram (David's father) in 2002, Mr. Bertram looked back to the buy-out, which at the time seemed ideal for his company.[33] They had a world market for paper-making machinery and he estimated that 50 percent of their production was for export: "We depended on that all the time," he said, recalling some of their long-term connections overseas, "for nearly all the paper-mills in India were British owned, with a head office in London." There were business connections all over the world, "indeed friendships, for we were on first-name terms," he said, recalling paper-mills in Australia, the Philippines, South Africa, Rhodesia, Canada, Germany and Algeria. "We were consultants to the Algerian Government, for example..."

Although these countries were producers and suppliers of wood pulp and bamboo, the raw materials for making paper, they relied on Bertram's for machinery and technical expertise. "The competition was becoming really fierce ... we were very busy at the time, so we bought Melville-Brodie's in Kirkcaldy – they did a lot for the Coal Board, like pit-head gears and such, though we made smaller stuff." Paper-making machinery may be regarded as "small" beside the massive pit-head machinery, but,

[33] The recording of James Bertram was made in 2002 by Sarah Bromage for SAPPHIRE, (Scottish Archive of Print and Publishing History Records), which is based at the Department of Lifelong Learning at the University of Edinburgh. For use of the material, and for access to the original sound-recording, thanks are due to Dr Bromage, at the University of Stirling, and to Prof. David Finklestein at the University of Edinburgh.

in the wider context of plant installation, it is still sizeable. More importantly, the Kirkcaldy company had been making machinery for mills for many years, and other paper-mills already relied upon Melville-Brodie's. James Bertram emphasised that the essential consideration before the buy-out was finding engineers capable of the precision needed for jobs where every single machine had to be custom-made to fit the plant: "No two factories were alike." Besides skilled engineers to make the machines, Bertram's also needed first-class fitters to install the machinery: "We'd send out a senior man, and the mills out there would do the installation under our instruction." The Melville-Brodie reputation stood the test on all counts, and the Bertram's buy-out seemed to have worked well for both management and employees.

As an apprentice, Dougie worked on some of the paper-making machines that went through Bertram's order books:

> The drawing would arrive, like this one, and that went through every stage o production at Melville-Brodie's, from the drawin office tae the patternmakers and so on. And so, all o us worked on this machine, custom-built tae order. Then when it was finished, the machine was tested in the factory, then dismantled, crated up, an shipped oot tae the customer. They could be going anywhere in the world, an the fitters were selected tae go wi them. Of course they worked aw the time there were away, so there would be no time for sight-seeing.

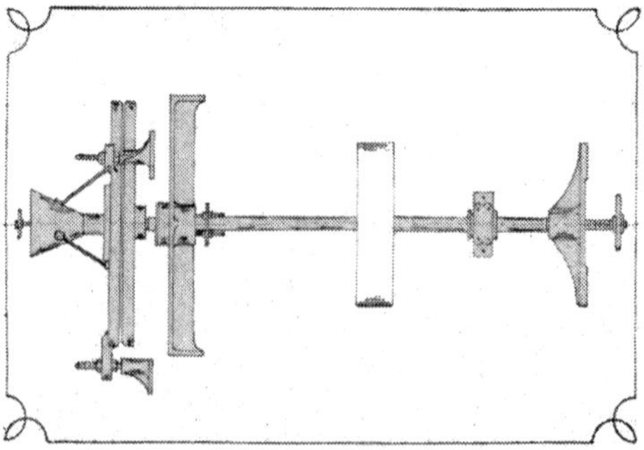

Machine drawing of a Haulage Guvernor 1930s.

High days, Holidays and Seeing in the Bells

Though the main holiday of the year was in summer, throughout the year there were occasional social events. Once in a while a dance was organised, though, as Willie recalled: "Sometimes the staff kept tae themselves, especially after the buy-out – maybe they didnae like mixin wi the workers, or they didnae fancy the dancin or maybe they werenae such good dancers as some o us!" Looking back on his life-long career with the firm, James Bertram spoke of the arm's length approach that was the norm for the family businesses. "The works day out was usually down the Clyde, and whole families would go," he recalled, adding that management "didn't really socialise with the workers." He also pointed out that the factories rarely closed down completely, as there was always maintenance to be done, and nobody took a holiday on Christmas Day.[34] Having worked for British Steel for many years, Dougie further explained: "In the steel works you have a shut-down period, where the equipment goes off in stages so you can maintain it," so a public holiday could be the ideal time to do this or to fit new plant, and have it inspected.

The phrase 'festive season' was yet to make an appearance in Scotland, and the big celebration of that time of year was Hogmanay. All over country this was the case, and folk looked forward to seeing in the New Year in their local, traditional way. As far as Christmas was concerned, anyone born before 1960 will recall a very different day from what has become the most commercial time of year. Back then, as Bob put it:

> You'd be so excited when you got an orange in the toe of your stockin, a wee chocolate Santa and maybe a wee toy. But that was only for children – you were out tae work at fourteen. Oh, Christmas was just another day at work. We got New Year's Day off but we didnae get Christmas. In my day, what the apprentices did, we aw had our own machines, an

[34] Recorded interview cited, 2002.

> we picked somebody else's machine, an we dressed it up. We put decorations an toys on it – just paper, like garlands. You just put stuff in the hole, an tied it, like my wee sister's toys an things, stuff they werenae usin. They did that every year. We had a lot o fun wi that, but of course you couldnae start work wi the decorations – you'd just have a laugh afore you'd get back tae normal. But I remember, there was one boy, he wouldnae touch it – he wasnae pleased! An the foreman had tae go an tell him, "Come on, lad, take it all in good part, an take it away, an get started." That was just on the day – oh aye, it was great fun.

It was similar in the Forties and Fifties, though by Drew's time there was no decorating machinery: "We worked Christmas, just the same, an got the first three days o the year off." That continued until the Sixties, when (possibly in the wake of the union involvement during the strike) the question of statutory holidays became a national issue. It was decided that there should be a one-day holiday during the festive season, but, as Scotland and England do not share the same traditions, it was inevitable that the choice would reflect the national customs. When the vote is proportional to the population density, however, the ratio leaves Scotland in a poor position.

Dougie remembers that Willie Black, who was their shop steward, played a key role in the discussion:

> We never used tae get holidays at Christmastime, an then all o a sudden there was tae be an agreement, nationally, that we would get one day o the seasonal year, (the festive season). Then, at the union meetin, there was one hellfire row got up because we had tae vote on what day we would take. It was a battle between Christmas Day an New Year's Day. There were folk from different nationalities worked at Melville-Brodie's, an some craftsmen wanted

> Christmas Day, some craftsmen wanted New Year's Day. An Willie Black was the Shop Steward, an he argued – and successfully argued – it wasn't just on this one, it was on the reduction o the workin week as well – Willie argued that the apprentices had a vote, 'cause they were aw members o the Union, so they had a vote. And, o course, some o the craftsmen thought that the apprentices would dae whatever Willie said – they knew that Willie wanted New Year's Day. But, as John said, the apprentices wanted New Year because they got more oot o it – for Christmas you used tae get an orange in your stockin! An we were used tae workin Christmas Day, so we kept New Year as the holiday, three days, then back tae work.

To the rest of the world, Christmas may have taken over, but the most popular Scottish tradition is still New Year. At Hogmanay, it's the sound of the bells, the strike of midnight with its count-down from twelve, the raised glasses, the first-footing, the black-bun, the lump of coal, the songs, music, dancing. They still agree that you have to see in the bells!

Did you know, however, there are no bell foundries in Scotland? Ronnie has the inside story, and being a foundry worker, he checked it out for himself – "You never know when somebody'll ask you to dae a bell."

> There is only one bell foundry that I know of in Britain, an that is doon in London, in Whitechapel. Aye, the same place where Jack the Ripper operated. It's probably the most famous one in the world – that's the one that cast Big Ben, the Liberty Bell, St Paul's Cathedral Bell – famous ones, like the Montreal Cathedral bell. They aw use the traditional method, so instead o usin a pattern, they use a sweep known as a *strickle*.[35] An it's the size an shape o the bell, an

[35] OED: tool used to shape sand or loam when making a mould for casting metal.

> it's pivoted on a spindle, an it's swung round as they pack the sand, an they sweep the strickle round tae give it the shape. An when they have that shape done, they line it wi clay, the thickness o the metal that they want the bell tae be, an then they repeat the process. Instead o the object revolvin, it's stationery. An when they've done the outer casin, they dry it in the furnace, an mount it on a big iron plate. Other sand is rammed roun aboot it tae make it more stable, an then when they lift that off, they can take the outer casin off, an remove the clay, so when they put it back on, a void is left where the clay was taken up. The clay gets broken up, tae remove it, so they pour the metal in. An every bell is unique – you have tae break the clay each time. Then after it's cast, it has tae be finished, both inside an outside.

Given the amount of metal that goes into making a bell (over 13 tons in Big Ben), moulders all recognise the importance of every stage of producing a bell to fit the requirement of its destination. It is also essential that it will sound good when it rings. Folk in every town will hear the church bell, for example, and as it takes a team of engineers to install it, Dougie explains that they too need to understand the process:

> The most important thing in makin bells is tae get the metal right, it's a special bronze known as 'bell bronze'. Big bells are prone tae crackin, even Big Ben is cracked, an the Liberty Bell, an the one in Russia, the Tsar Bell – they're aw cracked, an it's tae dae wi the shape o it, an what we called 'spring'. That happens when parts o it are contractin faster than other parts, an the metal tends tae spring it. But most bells are cast from old bells, so any old bells are sought after tae make new bells. If they can mend them, it would be cheaper, but there is also a demand for hand-bells. Aw the musical notes are related tae the different

> sizes o bells, an a bell has tae be tuned so it'll sound right. When the bell is cast, in order tae tune it, it's put in a large vertical lathe. An a copy o the strickle, a tool follows the shape, takes a certain amount o metal off, so the tuner gets that just spot-on.

A set of hand-bells in perfect pitch is the dream of every group of campanologists, and, as Dougie said, banjo-makers and players also value bell-bronze. For them, it's all to do with the tone ring. "The really *good* banjo-players will look for one made of bell-bronze. You can get one made of brass or wood, but bell-bronze will really make the banjo ring!"

For the lettering on large bells, however, it's back to the moulder, who has years of experience in the craft. Ronnie explains that, whatever the design, you start with the lettering in reverse:

> A lot o bells have letterin, so that has tae be stamped intae the mould, individually. Some o them are very ornate, so any decoration also has tae be stamped in reverse, an these ones can't be turned on the outside, it's the inside.

To make sure that every letter will face the right way, the moulder pays close attention to every detail. In his retirement Ronnie reflects on the craft that he has perfected over the years and still practices from time to time. His most recent moulds with lettering include the Melville-Brodie commemorative plaque, and a reproduction of the Melville-Brodie logo. As Ronnie aspires to fine craftsmanship, so also he appreciates the work of fellow foundry workers. Beside the back door of his house is one of his favourite examples of Kirkcaldy castings, an old, ornate bicycle stand like no other. Ronnie never tires of admiring it, and, as he turns to Dougie, he reminds him of the old ways: "It's a beautiful thing tae see a green sand mould, ready an waiting for the metal."

Ringing the Changes at Melville-Brodie Engineering Company

Although the making of bike-stands, musical instruments and church bells had never been part of the Melville-Brodie apprenticeship, one of the great satisfactions of the training was that the 'boys' became capable of adapting the skills they had learned. With the sense of achievement in becoming a journeyman came the excitement of finding a job. As Dougie explained, an engineering firm such as Melville-Brodie's would only have an opening on the retiral of one of their journeymen: "You would do a five year apprenticeship, and then you would look elsewhere for a job, which would leave room for another apprentice to come in." In the drawing office, Maureen's experience as a tracer (and the only girl) was much the same, though, at the time, nobody seemed to notice that there were significant gender differences:

> When I finished my apprenticeship in 1958, I was earning £5 a week. Then I had to look for another job – they didn't give you a rise, because they'd take in another apprentice to train; that was the system. But I got a training that was second to none; they'd trained me to do the most intricate engineering drawing imaginable, with the most miniscule fittings, all kinds of detail. More or less immediately I got a job with the Corporation in Glenrothes and I got a rise of thirty bob a week (£1.50 today), but the job wasn't nearly as interesting. I was tracing drawings for house plans and such, and none of the fine detail I'd been trained to do for the engineering drawings. The other option was to get a job with the Gas Board, but that doesn't have such detail either, so that's not so interesting. The other thing is, that after working for five years in Melville-Brodie's drawing office with all those boys, I could stand on my own two feet.

The main difference between the outcome for 'the boys' and the only girl apprentice at Melville-Brodie Engineering Company was that at the end of the five years the boys all had papers to show they had served the apprenticeship, whereas Maureen received nothing:

> Not a thing! That's just the way it was in those days, the girls didn't even get a piece of paper to show they'd done the full five-year apprenticeship and had satisfied all the requirements of it. But it wasn't just at Melville-Brodie's this happened, it was everywhere. The expectation was that you'd get married, so it wasn't so important – you'd stop working to be a wife and mother. In fact, I got married the following year, in 1959, but I worked on for a few years till my first boy was born. Women were also on a different pay scale to men, always less, even for the same work, and we didn't even question it, and in our department I was the only tracer so I wouldn't know if boys got paid more. So when I left to get another job, it was all word of mouth, and they trusted that. In a way, the piece of paper didn't matter so much to employers, because with the training we got at Melville-Brodie's they knew you could get a job anywhere, and I got another job no bother.

By the time apprentices engineers completed their training the boys were ready to make and fit machinery wherever it was needed. Dougie's career, which began with British Steel, took him to England, where he worked for thirty years, though he returned to Kirkcaldy to retire. Most of the engineers found jobs in Scotland's central belt, though several went overseas or became marine engineers.

When Matthew Morrison completed his apprenticeship, he moved to Edinburgh, where he worked for Johnson & Johnson, Co., a firm specialising in the manufacture of supplies for the health services. Very few doctors or nurses reaching for a disposable glove might think of how it is made, yet there would be no such thing were it not for designers such as Matthew. The product may be a far cry from paper-rollers or pit-head gears, but, as Matthew put it, "Engineering is engineering." Without such expertise there would be no dentistry chairs that recline to the perfect position, far less dental equipment or individually moulded dental implants; no customised hospital beds, never mind catheters; and have you thought about miniscule hearing aids? Matthew explained why a company making medical and surgical supplies would employ engineers:

> The machines that make those things have to be designed and made. My apprenticeship wi Melville Brodie stood me in good stead. In fact it always stood me in good stead – I started as an apprentice turner wi Willie Black, then after four years I went into the drawing office, and progressed to being a designer. The fact that I had started off on the shop floor was a huge advantage, because sometimes (in other firms) draftsmen and designers work away from the shop floor, and they don't understand the process of building the machines. If you've got that background, like they taught us at Melville-Brodie's, it's a tremendous asset. And I had both sides.

Matthew's explanation also addresses the concept of 'transferable skills' which, in recent years, has become an important consideration to educators focusing on training and employment.

At the end of his long career in Edinburgh, Matthew joined the group of retired Melville-Brodie engineers and was delighted to go to Kirkcaldy to be among them at the unveiling of the plaque in May 2014. The passing of time seemed of little significance as he stood among the 'Melville-Brodie boys': "Some I met two years ago, but some o them I haven't seen for fifty years." Beside Matthew was his daughter Claire, and, being the daughter of an engineer myself, I sensed that this was more than just a day off work, or a day out with Dad – he, after all, had moved to

Edinburgh before she was born. As Claire's own career is in Social Care, I wondered what it was that merited organising a day off work as well as child-care to attend the unveiling of a plaque?

> All my life I've heard my Dad talking about how he was trained – I was brought up on all the stories about Melville-Brodie's. Then, four years ago I did a course at college on Social Care and for our first essay, we all had to write on Values. So I wrote my essay all about my Dad's apprenticeship, and what the guys passed on to them in the workshop. The title of my essay was, "My Father's Work Ethics at Melville-Brodie Engineering Company" because the things you hear all your life become your own values: "If a job's worth doing it's worth doing well," and "Don't bother starting unless you mean to finish." And this is what I want to pass on to the next generations... Absolutely! My kids have got this already. We're already passing this on to them. Hard working work ethics. [laughs] They've got it!

As the generations trained by Melville-Brodie Engineering Company have either reached the age of retirement or passed away, they have lived through memorable changes. Conversations that begin, "It's not just Melville-Brodie's..." lead to discussion about the entire industry, world markets, changing technologies, economics, government schemes, privatisation, nationalisation, and so on. Listening to them, and (with their permission) recording conversations, there can be no doubt that the Melville-Brodie Retired Engineers have spent their lives cultivating what is now termed 'a lifelong approach to learning'. Open-minded, lively, curious, inventive and progressive, they represent what was once called 'the best of British engineering.'

Willie Black was among those fortunate to keep his job with Melville-Brodie Engineering Company when he finished his apprenticeship. "There was an openin for a journeyman," and

Willie remained there until retirement, teaching hundreds of apprentices. He firmly believed that the five-year apprenticeship was the best option and was not keen on any reduction in the time spent in training:

> After the war, there were a lot o people looking for jobs, an that's when the [government] made that 'semi-skilled' category. Well, as I looked at it in those days, and still do, why start people semi-skilled when you're bringing up apprentices?

He may have lost count of the number of engineers he trained at Melville-Brodie's, yet, at the age of ninety, Willie's quiet way still catches attention. His apprentices, now in their seventies and eighties, agree with him, and one of them responds, "Why indeed?" Another animated discussion begins, and the consensus is that, "it wasnae just aboot engineerin, the apprenticeship taught you skills for life."

Melville-Brodie Engineering Company had been a subsidiary of James Bertram's for only a few years when the company was faced with a series of challenges nobody had anticipated. To begin with, the introduction of computer technology had a significant impact on the paper-making industry and on the printing trade. Paper-mills in Britain, which had been Bertram's customers, were not replacing old machinery during the transition, and it was also becoming too expensive to repair or maintain existing machinery. As James Bertram put it, "They were letting it fall to pieces and rot, rather than replace it." Overseas trade was also diminishing, firstly when British-owned companies in India were taken over by highly-skilled Indian engineers, and soon afterwards when similar trends emerged in the wider continent of Asia. After more than a century of travelling the world to install custom-made paper-making machinery, Bertram's world market seemed to grind to a halt. As James Bertram recalled, "all of a sudden, they could build their own paper-mills, machinery and run it themselves, which Bertram's couldn't do."[36] The company soon realised that Bertram's needed to diversify, as the UK paper industry was "on it knees." Though Dougie and most of 'the boys' had moved elsewhere, Willie Black was kept on, continuing to train apprentices while staying abreast of developing methods of production. As Dougie put it, "They couldnae dae withoot him – he was really Bertram's main man."

Options to paper-making machinery were considered, as the Kirkcaldy manager David Bertram recalled, during a conversation with Dougie: "He told me that, without a doubt we could still have done linoleum machinery repairs, coal-minin work, and so on, because we had aw the drawins, an aw the patterns an we had the expertise." That had been the intention, Bertram explained, when in 1963 they secured a contract to provide a complete linoleum plant in Yugoslavia. Plans were drawn up, and "they even took on additional patternmakers to go with the job, but unfortunately there was a massive earthquake there, so it all went by the board."[37]

Without an export market, the industry was in trouble, and so, in an effort to move with the times, the following year (1964), Bertram's joined forces with an overseas company, 'The Modern Plastic Corporation' of Clifton, New Jersey. Ostensibly American, though owned by Nefertiti Holdings of Switzerland, they specialised in thermoplastic extrusion machinery. Initially the newly-formed company became known as 'The Modern Plastic Machinery Corporation (UK) Ltd.', but shortly afterwards was re-named Melville Plastics Machinery Ltd. It is interesting that the company, co- owned by Bertram's, decided to reinstate the name 'Melville', and before long, it became one of UK's leading exporters of this particular line. Aside from supplying British firms, Melville Plastics had a significant market in Europe and the Commonwealth. Although this diversification had given the firm a major boost, they 'kept a hand in' with the industry that

[36] James Bertram interview, 2002.

[37] During the 1963 earthquake approximately 1,070 people were killed, thousands were injured, and over 80% of the city of Skopje, (now the capital of Macedonia), was destroyed.

had been Bertram's family trademark for over a century: paper-making machinery.

In February 1967, the board made the decision to close the moulding shop in Kirkcaldy, ending over a century of castings and the training of apprentices. Later that year, as James Bertram recalled, there was discussion of amalgamation between the two Bertram firms (Leith and Edinburgh), but the decision was to retain the status quo. They agreed, however, to collaborate in areas that suited both, starting with a big contract to build a paper-mill in Algeria. Given the decline in overseas trade, they welcomed this huge job, and though it required major investment, the prospects were very good. In 1970, however, just when the plant was nearing completion, disaster struck when a flood destroyed all the electrics that had just been installed. Besides having to replace all the wiring and electrical fittings, a massive clean-up was required, as well as repairs and refitting of the plant machinery. There would be a long delay in completion, and if they waited for an insurance settlement the whole operation would grind to a halt. Time was of the essence, as, unfortunately for Bertram's, the Algerian contract stated that, if the job was not completed within the agreed time, the Bertram consortium would be responsible for running the mill site. The daily cost was estimated at several thousand pounds, which, over months, would prove impossible without a loan, and so the firm applied to the bank that had handled their finances over decades. James Bertram remembered how shocked they were at the response: "Suddenly the bank pulled the plug, so that was it." That same year, the co-owners of Melville Plastics, Nefertiti Holdings[38], withdrew their support, leaving no alternative but to appoint a provisional liquidator.

Despite best efforts to keep the Kirkcaldy firm going, it had to be sold. Reflecting on the turn of events, James Bertram concluded:

---

[38] It seems that all was not transparent when James Bertram went into partnership with what then appeared to be an American firm. The track record of Nefertiti Holdings of Switzerland indicates (on-line) a series of bankruptcy, and registration in several different countries.

> Melville-Brodie's went the same way as the Leith Company – it went under. It needn't have done so if it had been standing independently, but the problem was that Bertram's Ltd was a 20% shareholder concern... a very poor arrangement, so we couldn't extract Melville-Brodie from the Leith Walk company. If we hadn't had the tie-up, a public company as distinct from a private company, like Leith Walk, we would have just hived it off on its own, and it may have been still running – I don't know.[39]

In 1971, Melville's Plastics Ltd. was sold to a Yorkshire company that had a good reputation with the rapidly developing plastics industry – 'Plasticisers' from Drighlington, near Bradford. The new name of the Kirkcaldy company then became 'Plasticers Ltd', ending an identity with the name 'Melville', which had endured for over a century. Willie Black was among the engineers who was kept on, and though he worked in the familiar, old premises, he adapted his skills to new methods of production.

In June 1974 misfortune struck again, when an extensive fire destroyed a third of the factory. In spite of the damage, however, the company carried on until finally closed down in 1981. As it is not the purpose of this book to write a history of the industry or the evolution of a company, no more need be added regarding mergers, take-overs and buy-outs. Instead, we return to the personal narratives of the retired engineers, 'the Melville-Brodie boys', with a few final questions. The first may seem rhetorical, yet it is one that many folk ask: why would a group of engineers, who have had successful careers all over the world, still have this strong identity with Melville-Brodie Engineering Company? The short answer, to a man, is: "It's the apprenticeship training."

As Dougie said, "When you finished the five years, you got your apprenticeship papers and your union card, both pinned together. And with Melville-Brodie's name on the top, you could

[39] Recorded in 2002, it is interesting to hear James Bertram refer to the company as 'Melville-Brodie's' even though it had been over 40 years since the name had been in use.

go anywhere in the world to work for any engineering company." The apprenticeship background they share may date back more than half a century, yet it is still draws them together. It has become the context in which they discuss a range of successful, diverse, and even prestigious, careers. Without exception, the retired engineers emphasise the importance of training, from the very basics to the most intricate detail of every challenge. Ronnie refers to John's training to give an example of the range of skills developed, besides the more obvious ones of drawing and making patterns: "The thing is, patternmakers had all the disciplines in wood-working, they could turn their hand to any carpentry, the higher end of carpentry." John also had a fulfilling career, with an early promotion to a management position and latterly a new career in secondary school education. Still only in his mid-twenties, he undertook a three-year course in teacher training, graduating in Technical Education. John worked within the Scottish Education curriculum, and during those years he saw several school-leavers capable of going on to university to study for an engineering degree. While that brings great satisfaction to all school teachers, in terms of training skilled engineers, John could recognise that there was a 'down side':

> The bit that's missing is skill-training, which equips you for actual work, whereas classroom instruction trains pupils to pass exams. Nothing can replace the hands-on experience that the five-year apprenticeship gave us, and a job well done brings a lot of satisfaction. Youngsters today don't actually have the choice that we had, with its guarantee of five years of employment.

Job Satisfaction

No matter what the work may entail, both employers and employees are concerned with job satisfaction. It is not just a question of liking the job, or being content with the pay, as it affects company morale, stress level, family life, burn-out and general health. While the concept may not have been discussed widely as it is by today's career advisors, it was, nevertheless, at the heart of Willie Black's approach to training: he urged the less capable to think ahead, to imagine how life could be ruined by the wrong choice of job, and he kept an eye on the most promising apprentices. As Dougie recalled: "He wouldnae stand any nonsense," and the apprentices soon discovered for themselves, "it's much more satisfying to finish a job **you** could be proud of. Nobody could question you on what you'd done, and nothing could be questioned on your part of the job." From the point of view of the patternmakers, John agreed that, "There was a lot o satisfaction in the trade."

Considering, however, that Ronnie described his work in the foundry as being filthy, noisy, and at times horrible, the phrase 'job satisfaction' may not immediately come to mind. Yet, in retirement, Ronnie still keeps a hand in, and has even set up his own 'wee foondry' in his garage. When asked to take on a project, such as making engine parts for a First World War aeroplane, the fact that Ronnie lights up suggests he has considered job satisfaction, despite working in the most hostile conditions in any engineering company.

"Well, it's like this," Ronnie began, "Are you acquainted with Burns's poem, 'The Twa Dugs'?" A nod of reassurance, and Ronnie continues with his analogy. As a long-time member of the Auchterderran Jolly Beggars Burns Club, he makes his point more creatively than any definition of 'job satisfaction':

> One of the verses, you know the one, where Burns compares the way o the gentry against the working boy – on the one side, among the gentry, a dog, Caesar, is kept as a pet, and the other dog, Luath, is

a working collie. So Luath, who works hard aw day, gives his side o it, an says:

But will ye tell, me, Master Caesar,
Sure, great folk's life is a life o pleasure?
Nae cauld nor hunger e'er can steer them,
The very thought o't need na fear them..

Then you get the view o the gentry, when Caesar goes on to say it's no as easy as you think it is. For example, he says to Luath:

A country fellow at the pleugh,
His acres's till'd, he's right eneugh;
A country girl at her wheel,
Her dizzen's dune, she's unco weel;
But gentlemen, an ladies warst,
Wi' ev'n-down want o' wark are curst.
They loiter, lounging, lank an lazy;
Tho' deil-haet ails them, yet uneasy;
Their days insipid, dull, an tasteless;
Their nights unquiet, lang, an restless.

So, it's always been the way wi working folk – when they got their days work done, they were contented. And there's more to life than work – songs, music, poetry, vintage motor bikes... I can go fishin, camping ... in fact I've got the loch booked up near Dunkeld for Monday, an I go up in my wee camper van... a wee loch with just the one boat on it, so I have it to mysel. I can share the fish with otters and the ospreys, beautiful... I had a wee side-line, tyin artificial flies for the fishin, maistly starling wings, aw different patterns, Greenwells Glory, Kingfisher, Butcher, Silver Butcher, Murray Butcher, Dunkeld, Black Pennel, Victor, Zulu, Burn Fly.... Ocht aye.

In considering his day's work in the context of a week's work, or his week's work in the context of family and community life, Ronnie shares the bard's viewpoint: "It maks him quite forget his labour an his toil..."

As the story of Kirkcaldy's engineering industry began with the flax trade, it may be fitting to end this chapter of it with a verse from the ploughman poet, who grew flax, and also tried out an apprenticeship as flax-dresser:

> From scenes like these, old Scotia's grandeur springs,
> That mak her loved at hame, revered abroad;
> Princes an lords are but the breath o kings;
> An honest man's the noblest work o God![40]

[40] Both quotations are from Robert Burns's 'The Cotter's Saturday Night'.

Melville-Brodie years (W. Lindsay photos)

Engineers' outing – Station Hotel, Kirkcaldy, 9 April 1954. Left couple: Mr. & Mrs Wull Lindsay; Right hand couple: Mr. & Mrs Willie Black and friends at the works night out. Photography by David Ireland, 125 Commercial Street, Kirkcaldy.

Melville-Brodie outing – 21 May 1960, Pitlochry. Back row: 2nd L is Archie McGilvray, Walter Rymick (1st right back row), middle row, seated, George Brown and beside him (R) is Aund Farr (w. daughter), next to woman with beach ball is Willie Black seated front row with son.

Apprentices, Kirkcaldy, 1940s.

Break time on a sunny day, the boys in boilersuits, Junction Road, Kirkcaldy. Wull Lindsay (2nd left), 1953.

Melville-Brodie, journeymen and apprentices. Break time for the boys in boilersuits, 1953.

Melville-Brodie Engineers around a Medium centre lathe. L to R, sitting Gus, Robb, unkonwn, Wull Lindsay (3rd left), unkonwn, Will Mutch (2nd R) Willie Black (end R). Photo by James R. Smith. Professional Photographers, Rosslyn Street, Kirkcaldy, Fife. Phone 51655.

ref: 6/8157 - Centrifugal Pump: 18" diam. Impeller, M.S. spindle mounted on ball Bearing tex rope or direct coupled drive. Photo by Caithness Brothers. The Photographers; 100 Loughborough Road; Kirkcaldy.

Ref: 3004/3 Centre lathe with dividing heads. Dean Smith and Grace, Photographic Department, P.O. box 15, Keighley, Yorkshire, England.

Liquid pump made by Melville-Brodie Engineering, 1960s. Dean Smith and Grace. Photographic Department, P.O. box 15, Keighley, Yorkshire, England.

Ref: 3201/13r, Medium lathe with copy unit. Dean Smith and Grace. Photographic Department, P.O. box 15, Keighley, Yorkshire, England.

Ref: 3201/13 copy unit of the Dean Smith and Grace lathes. Dean Smith and Grace. Photographic Department, P.O. box 15, Keighley, Yorkshire, England.

Polishing machine with plane head. Melville-Brodie Engineering.

Polishing machine with plane head, Melville-Brodie, Kirkcaldy.

Machining keyway in extruder shaft.

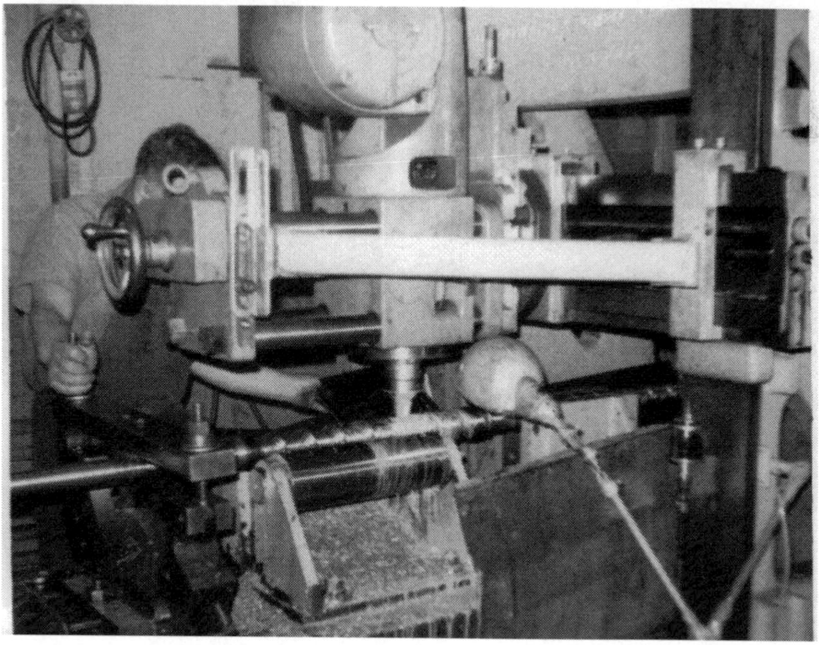

Machining keyway in extruder shaft.

Polishig plastics extruder screw.

Finish polishing extruder screw.

Ref: 2893/12 Compound drive.

Ref:2893/12. Compound slide drive (rear view) Dean Smith and Grace. Photographic Department, P.O. box 15, Keighley, Yorkshire, England.

UNVEILING MELVILLE-BRODIE PLAQUE, 14 MAY 2014

To commemorate the site of the engineering company that made such a major contribution to Kirkcaldy's industrial heritage and to the history of Scottish engineering.

APPENDICES

APPENDIX ONE

TIMELINE

The Melville Brodie Engineering Co.
Engineer's Iron Founders
Sinclairtown Foundry, Kirkcaldy
Established 1869 Operations Ceased 1981

1869 William Main Melville established the first company with iron founder Robert Henderson

1908 Melville & Henderson Engineers & Iron founders Dissolved. William Main Melville Sole Proprietor

1909 William Kilgour became Partner. Robert Burt Brodie became employed with Co. then became Partner in 1910

1918 William Main Melville. Business to be carried on by Robert Burt Brodie and Wm Kilgour, under the name of The Melville Brodie Engineering Co.

1921 Robert Burt Brodie became Sole Owner

1934 John Brodie appointed Director

1961 Melville Brodie Engineering Company became subsidiary of James Bertram & Son, Ltd., Leith

1964 Melville Brodie became Melville Plastics

1971 Melville Plastics (Scotland) Ltd wound up

1971 Plasticers Ltd., Family firm from Drighlington (nr Bradford) took over Melville Plastics

1974 Plasticers Ltd. MB machine Department destroyed by fire

1981 Plasticers Ltd sold up.

Compiled by D. Reid

APPENDIX TWO

NEWSPAPER CLIPS

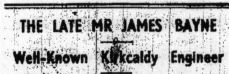

THE LATE MR JAMES BAYNE

Well-Known Kirkcaldy Engineer

It is with regret that we record in our columns to-day the death of Mr James Bayne, which occurred at his residence, Ponclair, Lady Nairn Avenue, Kirkcaldy, on Monday. The eldest son of the late Mr Charles Bayne, Dysart, he served his apprenticeship as an engineer with the late Mr W. M. Melville, Sinclairtown Foundry, now the Melville-Brodie Engineering Works. After about a year and a half with Messrs Milne, of Leith, followed by six months with the Kirkcaldy Linoleum Coy., where he worked the first printing machine introduced into the linoleum industry in Kirkcaldy, he returned to Sinclairtown Foundry to take up the post of chief draughtsman, and later, when the business was acquired by the Melville-Brodie Engineering Co., he was appointed manager, and held that appointment up till his death, a period of about twenty-five years, his total service at Sinclairtown Foundry being about fifty years.

He had a lifelong connection with Normand Road U.F. Church, Dysart, in which he held office as manager and elder, and for a number of years was preses of the congregation. Of a quiet and kindly disposition, he made many friends, and his passing is a distinct loss to the church.

The funeral, which took place to Dysart Cemetery on Thursday afternoon, was largely attended, the cortege including a large body of workers from Sinclairtown Foundry, the staff of which was also represented at the service in the house, which, as well as the service at the graveside, was conducted by Rev. G. W. F. Goodman, minister of Normand Road Church.

Mr Bayne, who was sixty-six years of age, leaves a widow and three sons—Mr Charles Bayne, chemist, Kirkcaldy; Mr James Bayne, headmaster, Kemback School; and Dr William Bayne, Kirkcaldy.

March 16, 1940, Dougie Reid archive

TWO REBUFFS FOR STRIKE COMMITTEE

Parents Support Employers

The Clydeside strike committee yesterday suffered a double rebuff when 400 journeymen employees of Kelvin and Hughes, scientific instrument makers, Hillington, Glasgow, decided not to take part in to-morrow's demonstration march in Glasgow, and parents of the firm's 53 apprentices agreed that their sons should return to work, probably to-morrow.

The parents met Mr Charles Baylis, works manager, and after a general discussion had an interview with three members of the strike committee. Payslips were produced showing that the 53 apprentices were already earning more money that that demanded by the strikers. When the youths of the strike committee left more than an hour afterwards one said:—"We had a rough handling. You would think it was a shareholders' meeting."

Mr Baylis told reporters:—"The youths have gone back to their committee to express the parents' case and there is a hope that our boys will be allowed to return to work on Wednesday. This is not to be regarded as a victory, but as a mutual arrangement."

In Edinburgh

At a meeting attended by about 200 apprentices in Edinburgh yesterday it was unanimously decided to call out the apprentices who, for reasons of hardship, have so far been allowed to remain at work. Some will receive money from the strike committee.

Efforts are being increased to get all the apprentices employed by Ferranti, Ltd., engineers, to join in the strike. Yesterday 30 of the 120 boys who had come out went back to work, and it was decided to increase the strength of pickets at the factory gates this morning.

Apprentices at a number of works in England yesterday joined the unofficial strike. A member of the strike committee in Manchester said last night that 5000 boys are on strike at 30 firms in the Greater Manchester area.

BOY STRIKERS TOLD TO RETURN

Unions' Advice on Eve of Pay Talks

FROM OUR INDUSTRIAL CORRESPONDENT: LONDON, Monday

Leaders of the Confederation of Shipbuilding and Engineering Unions to-night advised shipyard apprentices to return to work so that negotiations can proceed on their claims for improved wages in engineering and shipbuilding.

A message to that effect was sent to all affiliated unions and district committees after talks in which Mr Frank Foulkes, president of the Electrical Trades Union, and the chairmen of the confederation's sub-committee, including Mr E. J. Hill, secretary of the Boilermakers' Society, and Mr W. J. Cabron, president of the Amalgamated Engineering Union, took part.

Members of the executive council of the A.E.U. at Blackpool to-night decided that a circular instructing any young members on strike to return to work should be sent to the districts affected.

Earlier to-day the Shipbuilding Employers' Federation informed the confederation that, because of the strike, it would be wrong to discuss the application for an increase in apprentices', boys', and youths' wages at the meeting taking place between them on Friday.

The claim, could not be considered on Friday unless there was a complete return to work before then.

The employers explained that their decision not to discuss the claim with the confederation officials had been delayed until the last possible date in the hope that the unofficial strike would end.

Instead, apprentice delegates from Scottish areas had visited shipyards in the north-east of England and persuaded apprentices in a number of yards there to take strike action.

Attempts were still being made by apprentice delegates from Scotland to spread the strike to other shipbuilding districts.

SHARE IN INCREASES

Claims "Nonsensical"

An employer described as "nonsensical" claims made by the apprentices that there had been no wage advance in six years. They had shared on a percentage basis in each pay increase granted in the industry in national negotiations throughout that period, and in the award of a 42-hour week without loss of pay which was introduced on March 28.

The following tables show the present rates for a 42-hour week and the corresponding rates for a 44-hour week at April, 1954, and at May, 1952, when the basis of payment to apprentices was last agreed nationally:—

Apprenticeship Year	April 1960		April 1954		May 1952	
	s.	d.	s.	d.	s.	d.
First	63	1½	49	2	43	10
Second	74	10	57	5	50	9
Third	96	7	75	8	67	8
Fourth	113	4	88	11	79	7
Fifth	130	0½	102	2	91	6

At a conference in June, 1956, the employers rejected a claim on behalf of apprentices, boys, and youths employed in the shipbuilding and ship-repairing industry.

Until the present claim was intimated to the employers in the middle of March, no further claim had been advanced on behalf of apprentices, who have had their rates automatically increased on six occasions since the agreement reached in May, 1952.

Glasgow Herald, 3rd May 1960, front page

44 YOUNG STRIKERS ARRESTED

Incidents After Unofficial Parade of Apprentices

Forty-four Scottish apprentices who are on strike over a pay claim were arrested and charged with disorderly behaviour and forming part of a disorderly crowd yesterday after police broke up an unofficial march through Glasgow. Three vans took the youths to the Central Police Station. They were later released.

Earlier, an official parade with police escorts marched from Blythswood Square to Glasgow Green, where they were addressed by a member of the strike committee.

Most of the 500 apprentices who had taken part in the parade started to march back along Argyle Street, singing and shouting.

Some attempted to walk through a department store but a police cordon was thrown across the entrance. Traffic was halted as the strikers crossed Argyle Street into the Argyll Arcade, a covered shopping thoroughfare.

Squads of police sealed both entrances but some of the youths escaped. The others were detained until the arrival of the police vans.

At the Green no hands were raised when a call was made for strikers to do picket duty outside the premises of firms where apprentices are still working, and the inducement of money for cigarettes persuaded only half a dozen to volunteer to collect money for the strike funds.

Lobby Confederation

About 30 Scottish apprentices will be in York to-day when, with English apprentices, they hope to lobby members of the executive council of the Confederation of Shipbuilding and Engineering Unions and present their case to them. Telegrams will also be sent to the confederation from district branches of the unions in Scotland asking them to support the strike.

After a meeting in Glasgow yesterday of delegates from various parts of Scotland and England, a member of the strikers' committee said the delegation would ask the confederation to press for an early date for discussions with the employers.

Meanwhile an intensive campaign would be carried on in yards and workshops to collect money for the strikers.

A recall conference of delegate apprentices has been arranged for Saturday in Liverpool—the first time an all-Britain meeting has been held outside Glasgow since the start of the strike now in its third week.

LITTLE SUPPORT

Financial Strain

Apprentices on strike in Aberdeen at a meeting yesterday told their leaders that they were finding it hard to continue without money.

A member of the strike committee said it was estimated that more than 80 apprentices had recently gone back to work.

Several hundred journeymen employed by Anderson, Boyes and Co., Ltd., the Motherwell Bridge and Engineering Company, Ltd., and Associated Electrical Industries Ltd.—all of Motherwell — held a one-day token strike yesterday to support the apprentices.

Journeymen, apprentices, and about 50 girls, a total crowd of 2000, attended a demonstration in the town.

Glasgow Herald, 12 May 1960, front page

APPRENTICES MAY END STRIKE

Unions Order Return to Work to Help Negotiations

The apprentices strike should end this week-end. Leaders of the 40-union Confederation of Shipbuilding and Engineering Unions yesterday ordered a return to work so that negotiations can be opened with the employers' organisations on the boys' claim for a higher pay rate.

Sixty apprentices from Scotland, Tyneside, and Merseyside who lobbied the union leaders at a York meeting yesterday heard that the confederation's executive council had passed a resolution placing full blame for the dispute on the employers.

The resolution, said Mr Frank Foulkes, chairman, blamed the employers "because of their continual refusal to improve percentages (of the adult rate) and accede full negotiating rights for apprentices.

"Having received assurances that there will be no victimisation," the resolution stated, "the confederation reaffirms its previous recommendation to trades unions to take appropriate steps to have their members resume normal working to facilitate early negotiations."

While a deputation of three apprentices was engaged in talks with the executive council, a confederation spokesman was telephoning the employers to arrange dates for the meetings: May 20 was fixed with the shipbuilding employers, and the engineers are believed to be prepared to meet the union negotiators before the month ends.

After yesterday's meeting most of the Scottish apprentices present said they were happy to go back to work, having made their point; the Merseyside boys have arranged a mass meeting in Liverpool to-morrow.

It is clear, from a meeting of officers of the confederation's 48 district committees which followed, that the union leaders are going to have to accept some alteration to their general policy on working the shorter week gained in March.

The meeting was held to discover the feelings of members and no policy action was taken. But it was obvious from speaker after speaker that the rank-and-file members of the unions are determined not to spread the 42-hour week over five equal shifts, as agreed between their leaders and the employers.

The new general pattern already applied by nightshift workers in the Midlands motor and engineering industries is four nine-and-a-half hour shifts and a four-hour spell on Fridays.

There is even one firm proposal by the National Union of Vehicle Builders which will come up for discussion at the confederation's annual conference at Llandudno in July for a four-day week of 38 hours without loss of pay.

This goes right against the elder union leaders' 50-year fight for a shorter working day, but the decision will rest with the men on the workshop floor.

Members of the Clydeside apprentices' committee gave no indication yesterday when a full resumption of work might take place. They are waiting for the report from their delegates who are returning from York to Glasgow to-day to attend a meeting of the strikers.

No decision about ending the strike, however, is likely to be made until to-morrow, when apprentices from all over Great Britain meet in Liverpool.

Indications are that the majority of Clydeside apprentices will welcome a general return to work.

Glasgow Herald, 13 May 1960, front page

APPRENTICES MAY DECIDE TO-DAY

Unions' Call for Return to Work

Shipyard and engineering apprentices from all over Britain who have been on strike for nearly three weeks over a pay claim are meeting in Liverpool to-day to discuss instructions from their unions to return to work immediately so that negotiations may open with the employers' organisations.

Fifty delegates representing Scottish apprentices left for Liverpool last night. A spokesman for the Clydeside delegates said they had "definite proposals" concerning the call to return to work

Confederation of Shipbuilding and Engineering Unions.

The apprentices are on strike in support of their demand for wage increases of up to £2 12s 6d a week.

On Monday morning the strike committee will meet Clydeside shop stewards "to discuss organisation," and a mass meeting is to be held at Glasgow Green in the afternoon.

Vote for Return

Representatives of the 11,000 engineering apprentices on strike in the greater Manchester area decided at Manchester yesterday to recommend a return to work on Monday morning. They reaffirmed their intention to "continue the dispute if the answer of the employers is unsatisfactory."

Some 800 of the 1100 apprentices employed at the Birkenhead shipyard of Cammell Laird and Co., Ltd., decided yesterday to return to work on Monday.

Glasgow Herald, 14 May 1960, front page

(1)

Kirkcaldy Engineering Firm Plan To Extend

Construction work is likely to start in the early spring on a large new engineering factory at Kirkcaldy's Hayfield industrial site.

The firm contemplating expansion are the Melville Brodie Engineering Company, Sinclairtown Foundry, Kirkcaldy, a subsidiary of James Bertram & Son Ltd., Leith.

Last night they received approval in principle from the Town Council's Planning Committee for the acquisition of upwards of 20 acres at the industrial site, and the firm particularly ask that the matter be expedited to let them get ahead swiftly with the project.

Councillor A. Dingwall, planning convener, said today: "Kirkcaldy has been losing out a little industrially with the closure of a number of linen mills, and for that reason this news of new industry is all the more welcome.

FOR INDIA ?

"While details of the firm's plans have yet to come before us, one can assume that a request for so much ground will eventually lead to a factory employing several hundred people when fully developed. The fact that it is engineering work also indicates a fair amount of employment, for it is not the type of project that will call for extensive storage romm. Most of the space will be for use as the factory floor where me nwill be at work."

While the management at the Sinclairtown foundry wiuld make no official comment today, it was being widely rumoured in Kirkcaldy that at least part of the new factory's output will be concerned with papermill machinery for the Indian market. This would represent something of a commercial "come back" for Kirkcaldy, which at one time produced machinery for Indian rice and hemp mills.

8179

FIFE FREE PRESS, SATURDAY, FEBRUARY 25, 1

Moulding Shop Closes Down

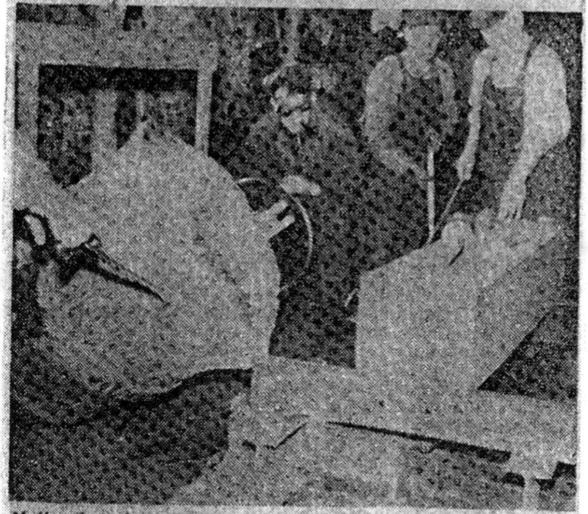

Molten iron is cast into a mould at the Sinclairtown Foundry of James Bertram & Son Ltd., formerly the Melville Brodie Engineering Co. The production of castings ended this week and the moulding shop will now be used for engineering work. The moulders and pattern-makers have all been offered other jobs in Edinburgh.

8180

Bertrams Ltd
Successors to Geo & Wm Bertram
Established 1821
Engineers
St Katherine's Works
Sciennes & Leith Walk
Edinburgh
& Westfield Foundry

- Sam

Fife Free Press, 25 February 1967. Dougie Reid archive

130 JOBS ARE AT STAKE

THE Kirkcaldy firm of Melville Plastic Machinery Ltd.—one of the leading exporters of plastics extrusion machinery from the United Kingdom—are to go into voluntary liquidation.

The owners of the company, Nefertiti Holdings of Switzerland, have withdrawn their support.

Mr David Bertram, a director of Melville Plastics, said: "The company has applied for the appointment of a provisional liquidator to take effect from the end of this week or the beginning of next week."

The firm has a payroll of about 130 staff and employees.

Mr Bertram said: "We don't know what the position will be with the employees at the moment.

"This will be up to the provisional liquidator when he arrives.

"But we are confident of the 'know-how' that the company has and that it is a saleable entity.

"We hope that a suitable purchaser will come forward and buy the company as a going concern.

"We are hopeful for the future of the employees."

Melville Plastics were formerly the Melville Brodie Engineering Company, a long-etsablished firm which had been in business in Kirkcaldy for over 100 years.

They began manufacturing plastics extrusion machinery seven years ago at their Sinclairtown Foundry at Junction Road.

In 1961 the company, then a subsidiary of papermill engineers James Bertram & Son Ltd. of Leith, announced plans to erect a new factory at Kirkcaldy's Hayfield Industrial Estate.

The project, it was said, would ultimately provide employment for about 500, and the company proposed to develop about 18½ acres of land as a heavy engineering works and iron and brass foundry.

But the plans eventually came to nothing.

Earlier this year, Melville Plastics exhibited some of their machinery at the Johannesburg Plastics Exhibition and only two weeks ago, they took part in a huge international plastics fair in Dusseldorf.

Fife Free Press, Friday 1 October 1971, Dougie Reid Archive

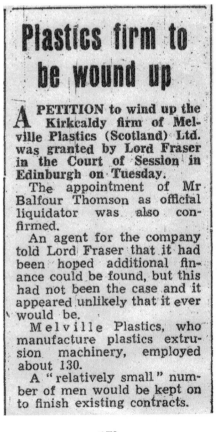

Plastics firm to be wound up

A PETITION to wind up the Kirkcaldy firm of Melville Plastics (Scotland) Ltd. was granted by Lord Fraser in the Court of Session in Edinburgh on Tuesday.

The appointment of Mr Balfour Thomson as official liquidator was also confirmed.

An agent for the company told Lord Fraser that it had been hoped additional finance could be found, but this had not been the case and it appeared unlikely that it ever would be.

Melville Plastics, who manufacture plastics extrusion machinery, employed about 130.

A "relatively small" number of men would be kept on to finish existing contracts.

10/6/74

Kirkcaldy factory blaze

DAMAGE EXCEEDS £250,000 – BUT JOBS ARE SAFE

Left: Onlookers watch as part of the factory roof collapses at the height of the blaze, which gutted an extensive section of the premises. Below: The full extent of the damage is seen in this picture taken on Tuesday morning.

The jobs of the complete work-force at the Kirkcaldy factory of Plasticisers Ltd. are safe – despite the disastrous fire on Monday evening which reduced almost a third of the premises to a charred shell.

Only minutes after the firm's 80 employees clocked off for the day, the store-room and machine shop of the building in Junction Road were transformed into a blazing inferno.

Firemen, fortunately, managed to confine the outbreak to this section, saving some 70 per cent of the factory from fire damage and preventing the flames from spreading to the neighbouring maltings of Robert Kilgour & Co. Ltd.

At the height of the blaze, families in adjoining Kidd Street, were warned to prepare for evacuation, but this, in fact, proved unnecessary.

Officials from the firm's headquarters in Drighlington, near Bradford, were on the spot less than 24 hours later, after flying by private plane to Glenrothes and then motoring to Kirkcaldy, to assess the damage.

An initial assessment of the situation put the estimated cost at between £250,000 and £500,000.

The firm's chairman, Mr I. D. Slack, confirmed there was no danger of any redundancies, and that production would continue to a limited extent.

"There is no question of anyone being laid off," he said.

As soon as electricity was restored to the factory within a couple of days, he expected output to reach 70 per cent of normal production capacity.

The firm have meanwhile rented accommodation outside the burgh to help with some of the work, until a decision is made on the future of the Junction Road building.

Mr Slack said: "I would like to pay tribute to all the local engineering firms who have offered every kind of assistance – from space to machinery, and even offers to do work for us.

"The response has been tremendous and I can't thank them enough."

Mr Slack said that, fortunately, most of the plastic processing equipment being manufactured by the firm was not in the section severely damaged, and there was no danger of their failing to honour contracts.

WEEK'S DELAY

The factory manufactures equipment for customers all over the United Kingdom.

"There will be about a week's delay," said Mr Slack, "but our main problem is storage space.

"Our premises in East March Street, which were under demolition order, will be resurrected as a temporary store-room."

The blaze was first spotted shortly after five o'clock by Mr Andrew Christie, an employee of the firm, as he was checking and locking up the factory for the night and he immediately raised the alarm.

Four units of Fife Fire Brigade, plus a snorkel, were quickly on the scene and attacked the blaze which had taken a firm hold of the building.

Road blocks and diversions in the area caused havoc with the peak-hour traffic, and the huge pall of smoke could be seen over a wide area.

Passers-by and employees who had just left the factory, watched as the roof of the centre section of the building collapsed and, four hours later, the remains of the machine room still smouldered.

On Wednesday, a local demolition firm began clearing up the debris and making the building safe, and the Junction Road end of Beatty Crescent, which flanks the side of the factory, was still blocked off.

Fife Police and the Fire Brigade are continuing their investigations into the cause of the outbreak, and a report will be submitted as soon as possible to the Procurator Fiscal at Kirkcaldy.

Plasticisers Ltd., which was founded in 1940 and is part of a family business stretching back to 1750, came to Kirkcaldy in 1971.

They took over the premises in Junction Road after the liquidation of the former occupants, Melville Plastics (Scotland) Ltd., who manufactured similar equipment.

[illegible] some 80 employees on their payroll at Kirkcaldy, including 50 engineers, labourers and office staff.

Fife Free Press, 10 June 1974, Dougie Reid archive

REPRINTED FROM FIFE DIRECT

Proposed Memorial to Melville Brodie Engineers, Sinclairtown Foundry £2,000
Organisation: Reunion Retired Ex-Employees Group

To erect a memorial to the above company which was founded in 1869 & met it's demise in 1974. A reunion of ex-employees held primarily because of the com-plete lack of local historical records of such a successful company, both in terms of of the engineering products it made and the very skilled craftsmen it produced. Many of these are now spread all over the world. This memorial is particularly for the benefit of the Kirkcaldy community.

MAY 13, 2012 – FIFEDIRECT

REUNION is being held for former employees of a Kirkcaldy engineering firm.

The gathering will take place at the KUSI Club for the men and woman who worked at the Melville-Brodie Engineering Co Ltd which was situated on Junction Road.

Dougie Reid (70), who has organised the event, began working as an apprentice in 1957 and says it was a "marvellous" place to work.

"The skills you learned there were invaluable," he said.

"It took time though, you can't learn a new skill overnight.

"We would make parts for the fitters at other local companies like Nairns or Tullis Russell and you would find out that a lot of them had served an apprenticeship at Melville-Brodie.

"That was the norm back then.

Moved on

"You would do a five year apprenticeship and then you would look elsewhere for a job which would leave room for another apprentice to come in."

Dougie's own working career saw him ending up working in England for British Steel for 30 years before returning to Kirkcaldy.

And now he has plans to put together a publication about his former employers.

He said: "I had a look around and could hardly find anything about it.

"It would be a shame if it was forgotten about because it was a very important firm for Kirkcaldy at the time.

"I'm hoping to put together a book about it or maybe a website.

War time

"I think it's important that the younger generation learns about the past."

Willie Black (87) is another former employee who began as an apprentice in 1940.

"When I began it was during the war," he said. "We were making parts for aircraft carriers.

"After I finished my apprenticeship I stayed on and the firm was taken over by Bertam's a paper mill from Edinburgh."

The firm underwent another change of hands before it was destroyed by fire in the early 80s and now Willie is hopeful that the reunion will be a success. "It would be nice to catch up with people that I haven't seen for years," he said.

Dougie said: "Obviously a lot of the older craftsman may have passed away by now but if their relatives came along to share any memories that would be great."

The Melville Brodie reunion will be held at the KUSI Club, St Brycedale Avenue on Tuesday May 22 from 5.00 p.m. Call Dougie on 722302.

FifeToday
Glenrothes Gazette News
St Andrews Citizen News
Fife Herald News
Fife Free Press News
East Fife Mail News

08/01/15 | 3°C to 6°C Cloudy | Like us | Follow us | Place your Ad | Subscribe

Local Headlines | Scottish Headlines | Showbiz | Columnists | Public Notices | Emags | Health

Glenrothes | Levenmouth/East Fife | St Andrews/Cupar | Kirkcaldy/B'island | D'fermline/West Fife

Memorial to recall Kirkcaldy's industrial past

The memorial is unveiled

by Paul McCabe
paul.mccabe@jpress.co.uk

Published on the 22 May 2014 10:45

A permanent memorial to a mostly forgotten part of Kirkcaldy's industrial past was unveiled this week.

A bronze plaque has been erected at the Corner of Maltings Road and Junction Road, where the huge Melville-Brodie Engineering Company works stood for over 100 years.

The company which opened the foundry in 1869 finally closed its doors in 1981 and a group of former employees have been working hard to make sure that future generation of Langtonians are aware of Kirkcaldy's rich industrial heritage.

Dougie Reid formed the Retired Melville-Brodie Club five years ago and said it had been a very emotional day.

He said: "I never thought when we started off that we would be able to achieve this."

Among those present at the unveiling were John Greig, the last apprentice pattern maker to qualify, and Ronnie Fleming, the last apprentice moulder. Both had helped in the construction of the memorial.

APPENDIX THREE

Summary of Holdings of Melville-Brodie planning applications in Fife Archives[1]

Date: 19 July 1898
Reference: DG/K/5/4
Title: Sinclairtown Foundry, Overton Road, Kirkcaldy
Applicant: W M Melville
Description: new offices
Architect: 143 Back Street, Pathhead

Date: 10 September 1900
Reference: DG/K/1/303
Title: Sinclairtown Foundry, Overton Road, Kirkcaldy
Applicant: [Sinclairtown Foundry]
Description: Build a gas engine house and toilets
Architect: William Melville, engineer

Date: 14 April 1902
Reference: DG/K/1/403
Title: Sinclairtown Foundry, Factory Road, Kirkcaldy
Applicant: W M Melville
Description: Extension to engineers workshop

Date: 25 February 1904
Reference: DG/K/1/533
Title: Junction Rd, Kirkcaldy
Applicant: Steland and Wishart Ltd, Maunfacturers
Description: Alteration to engine house
Architect: W M Melville and Henderson, Engineers

---

[1] Fife Council Archives Catalogue <www.onfife.com/libraries-archives/archives/catalogue-search#>.

Date: 7 July 1925
Reference: DG/K/1/1625
Title: corner of Beatty Crescent and Overton Road
Applicant: Sinclairtown Foundry,
Description: build extension to fitting shop and dressers shed

Date: 3 September 1929
Reference: DG/K/1/1903
Title: Sinclairtown Foundry, Overton Road, Kirkcaldy
Applicant: The Melville Brodie Engineering Co
Description: build shed in Old Saw Mill

Date: 15 October 1929
Reference: DG/K/1/1919
Title: Overton Road, Kirkcaldy -Sinclairtown Foundry
Applicant: Melville Brodie Engineering Co
Description: build a garage in the Old Saw Mill

Date: 3 December 1929
Reference: DG/K/1/1926
Title: Overton Road, Kirkcaldy -Sinclairtown Foundry
Applicant: Melville Brodie Engineering Co
Description: extension to fitting shop
Architect: Andrew Fraser

Date: 19 November 1936
Reference: DG/K/1/2487
Title: Overton Road, Kirkcaldy
Applicant: Melville Brodie Engineering Co
Description: erect a pattern store

Date: 7 May 1942
Reference: DG/K/1/2819
Title: Junction Road/Beatty Crescent
Applicant: Melville Brodie Engineering Co
Description: erect additional lavatory accommodation

Date:	15 April 1948
Reference:	DG/K/1/3193
Title:	Sinclairtown Foundry, Junction Road, Kirkcaldy
Applicant:	Melville and Brodie Engineering Co
Architect:	Welsh and Hutchon, Kirkcaldy

Date:	01 September 1949
Reference:	DG/K/1/3296
Title:	Overton Road Sinclairtown Foundry
Applicant:	The Melville Brodie Eng Co
Description:	extension dressing shop at the Foundry

Date:	21 November 1957
Reference:	DG/K/1/6728
Title:	Junction Road, Kirkcaldy
Applicant:	Melville and Brodie Engineering Co
Description:	Erect roof over part of yard.

Date:	6 June 1961
Reference:	DG/K/1/4457
Title:	East March Street, Kirkcaldy
Applicant:	Melville and Brodie Engineering Co
Description:	Office extension

Date:	19 August 1965
Reference:	DG/K/1/5090
Title:	Beatty Crescent ,Kirkcaldy
Applicant:	Melville and Brodie Engineering Co
Description:	Demolish existing toilets & build new ablutions block

Date:	1 September 1966
Reference:	DG/K/1/5245
Title:	13, Overton Road, Kirkcaldy
Applicant:	Melville and Brodie Engineering Co
Description:	Demolish property

APPENDIX FOUR

INDENTURE
James Bayne, 20 September 1926

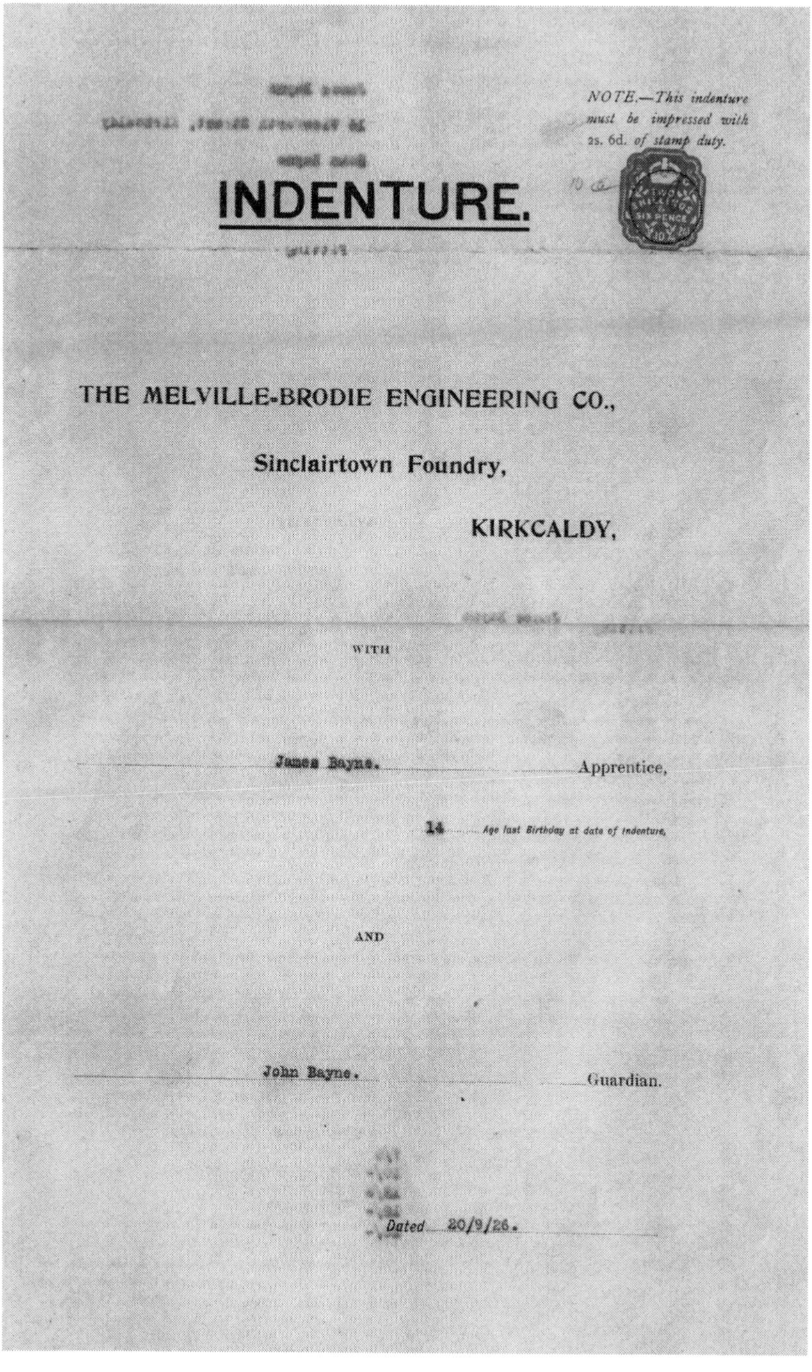

NOTE.—This indenture must be impressed with 2s. 6d. of stamp duty.

INDENTURE.

THE MELVILLE-BRODIE ENGINEERING CO.,

Sinclairtown Foundry,

KIRKCALDY,

WITH

James Bayne. Apprentice,

14 *Age last Birthday at date of Indenture,*

AND

John Bayne. Guardian.

Dated 20/9/26.

1. **It is Agreed** BETWEEN THE MELVILLE-BRODIE ENGINEERING CO., SINCLAIRTOWN FOUNDRY, KIRKCALDY

(hereinafter called "The Employers"), of the first part, and **James Bayne**

(hereinafter called "The Apprentice"), residing at **16 Viewforth Street, Kirkcaldy**

of the second part, with consent of **John Bayne**

(hereinafter called "The Guardian"), of the third part, as his curator and administrator in law, in manner herein stated, THAT IS TO SAY:—

2. BINDING: The Apprentice of his own free will, with consent of the Guardian, hereby puts and binds himself as a Trade Apprentice with and to the Employers in the **Fitting** Department of their business subject to the provisions herein for the full and complete space of five years. The Apprentice and the Guardian bind themselves jointly and severally, that during the continuance of this indenture the Apprentice shall industriously and faithfully serve the Employers and promptly obey all the lawful rules, regulations, and commands of the Employers, and of their officers, representatives and authorised employees, and shall conceal and in no ways reveal the secrets of the Employers' business or of the business of their customers, and also that the Apprentice will not do or commit, or suffer to be done or committed, any waste, damage or other injury to the property or goods of the Employers, and will not lend such property or goods to any person without the consent of the Employers.

3. PROBATIONARY PERIOD: Of the aforementioned period of five years, the first three months is to be regarded as a probationary period in that if the Employers shall find that the Apprentice is not likely to prove suitable for training as a Trade Apprentice, it shall be competent to the Employers to discharge said Apprentice, and contrariwise, if the said Apprentice finds that the trade to which he has put himself is not to be suitable, through ill-health or any other satisfactory reason which can be proved, it shall be competent for the Guardian to withdraw said Apprentice from such engagement, failing which the aforementioned period of three months having been served, it shall be understood that this Agreement is binding for the full period of five years.

4. REGULARITY AND ATTENTION: The Apprentice shall be regular and punctual in his attendance, well behaved and attentive to all instructions given him and shall behave himself civilly and respectfully to his Employers and their customers: and the Guardian shall discharge the whole obligations incumbent upon him in virtue of this indenture.

5. EMPLOYERS TO INSTRUCT THE APPRENTICE: FOR WHICH CAUSES AND ON THE OTHER PART the Employers agree to take the said **James Bayne** as their Apprentice during the said period in the **Fitting** Department of their business on the conditions of this indenture; moreover, the Employers bind themselves to instruct, or cause to be instructed, in so far as they reasonably can do so, the said Apprentice in the handicraft of the said Department and the requisite knowledge of the trade appertaining thereto, and the Apprentice shall use all the diligence and ability of which he is capable to become proficient therein.

6. HOURS PER YEAR: It is declared that each year of the apprenticeship shall consist of 2350 hours, or the statutory number of hours which may hereafter be laid down by law, and that no year shall be held to be completed until that number of hours in the year in question has been served by the Apprentice.

7. OVERTIME: The Apprentice shall, when necessary at the request of the Employers, and subject to the Factory Acts and any other Act for the time applicable to the Employers' business, work overtime. Declaring, however, that each hour of overtime worked by the Apprentice shall count as one hour and one-half, and each hour worked by the Apprentice on Sundays shall be reckoned as two hours.

8. OUTSIDE WORK. The Employers may require the Apprentice to work on the premises or at any place within Great Britain or Ireland where they happen to be employed.

9. LEAVE-OFF HOLIDAYS: The Apprentice shall not absent himself from the Works except on leave first asked and obtained from the Foreman in charge of his Department, but the Apprentice shall be allowed all usual Public or Trades Holidays observed in the Works before counting loss time falling to be made up.

10. In case the Apprentice shall be absent owing to illness, a Doctor's or Guardian's letter, satisfactory to the Employers, must be sent to the Works, failing which absence shall be considered absence without leave, unless an explanation satisfactory to the Employers is given.

11. No payment shall be due during any period the Apprentice is absent through sickness or on holiday or from any other cause, nor for any time lost on account of the closure of the Works for any cause.

12. PENALTY FOR ABSENCE: And should the Apprentice absent himself for any cause without leave, except through sickness or accident, he shall be liable to pay as liquidated damages the sum of 2s. 6d. for each day, and further, each hour of such absence shall be made up by one and a half hours' extra service.

13. RATES OF PAY: The Employers agree to pay the Apprentice for each week of actual duty performed and proportionately for less or more in accordance with the terms of this indenture and in compliance with such rules, regulations, and commands as the Employers may from time to time prescribe, the following sums respectively:—

For the First Year	**7/6**	Shillings per week.
For the Second Year	**10/-**	Shillings per week.
For the Third Year	**12/6**	Shillings per week.
For the Fourth Year	**15/-**	Shillings per week.
For the Fifth Year	**20/-**	Shillings per week.
For the Sixth Year		Shillings per week.

Declaring that if the Apprentice shall be employed out of the Works an extra weekly allowance shall be paid to him according to the usual custom of the Employers in such cases. And declaring that no payment shall be due for any period he is absent whether through sickness or on holiday or from any other cause, nor for any time lost on account of the closure of the Works for any cause.

10A. In case of allowance for illness, not more than six weeks in any one year to be allowed as time counted for Apprenticeship. This also applies to accidents outwith employers' control. In case of accidents in employers' works and for which compensation is paid, notemore than eight weeks in any one year will be counted as time served, except under special arrangement.

14. TRADE DISPUTE: The Apprentice shall not take part in any way in any labour dispute the Employers may have with any of their employees, but shall perform during the continuance thereof such work as he may be required to perform in the execution of his duties by the Employers.

15. DISMISSAL OR SUSPENSION: The Employers reserve the right to suspend for such time as they think fit, or to dismiss the Apprentice summarily without notice or compensation to Apprentice or Guardian, and to annul or cancel his indenture for any breach thereof or of the lawful rules and regulations of the Employers for the time, or for any misbehaviour, disobedience, or unfaithfulness on the part of the Apprentice towards the Employers or their foresaids, of which the Employers shall be the sole judges.

16. PAY DAYS: All monies earned by the Apprentice hereunder shall be paid to him on the regular pay days of the Employers as the same may from time to time be established, subject to any deductions that require to be made by law.

17. INTERRUPTION: The Employers will not be responsible for any interruption or stoppage of this indenture due to causes beyond their control.

18. CLASSES: The Apprentice will attend such classes as may be provided by the local Education Authorities for Technical Instruction, or by the Employer himself on his own premises.

19. CHANGE TO ENGINEERING APPRENTICESHIP: Notwithstanding anything herein stated as in Clause 2, it shall be optional for the Apprentice at any period up to the expiry of his fourth year of apprenticeship to apply to the Employers to be transferred to the General Engineering Section of their apprenticeship, under which he shall, if the Employers are satisfied that he is duly qualified, be permitted to serve a complete engineering apprenticeship of six years, thereby giving him the privilege of serving in two Departments of the Employers' business, with the opportunity under competitive conditions, of obtaining entry into the Employers' Drawing Office.

20. The Employers shall be entitled to put an end to this indenture should they cease to carry on business and that without being liable for damages.

IN WITNESS WHEREOF these presents are subscribed by the parties hereto at Kirkcaldy this 22nd day of September 1926, in the presence of the witnesses hereto subscribing.

Execution by the Employers.
THE MELVILLE-BRODIE ENGINEERING Co.
[redacted]

(Signature) James Hepburn,
(Designation) Clerk,
(Address) 15 Institution Street,
Kirkcaldy

(Date) 27/9/26

Signed by the Apprentice in the presence of:—

Signature of Apprentice.

(Signature) David Martin
(Designation) Labourer
(Address) 14 Viewforth Street

James Bayne
(Date) 25th Sept 1926

Signed by the Guardian in the presence of:—

Signature of Guardian

(Signature) Hugh Davidson.
(Designation) Motor Driver.
(Address) 70 Sutherland Street

John Bayne
(Date) 25th Sept 1926

ENDORSEMENT ON COMPLETION OF INDENTURE.

The terms and conditions of this indenture have been completed to our satisfaction.

THE MELVILLE-BRODIE ENGINEERING Co.

(Signature) R.M. Brodie. (Employers).

Date 19-9-31.

INDENTURE.

Messrs. The Melville-Brodie Engineering Co.,

SINCLAIRTOWN FOUNDRY,

KIRKCALDY,

WITH

James Bayne Apprentice.

AND

John Bayne Guardian.

DATED 20th September 1926.

APPENDIX FIVE

INDENTURE
Robert Thomson, 14 January 1935

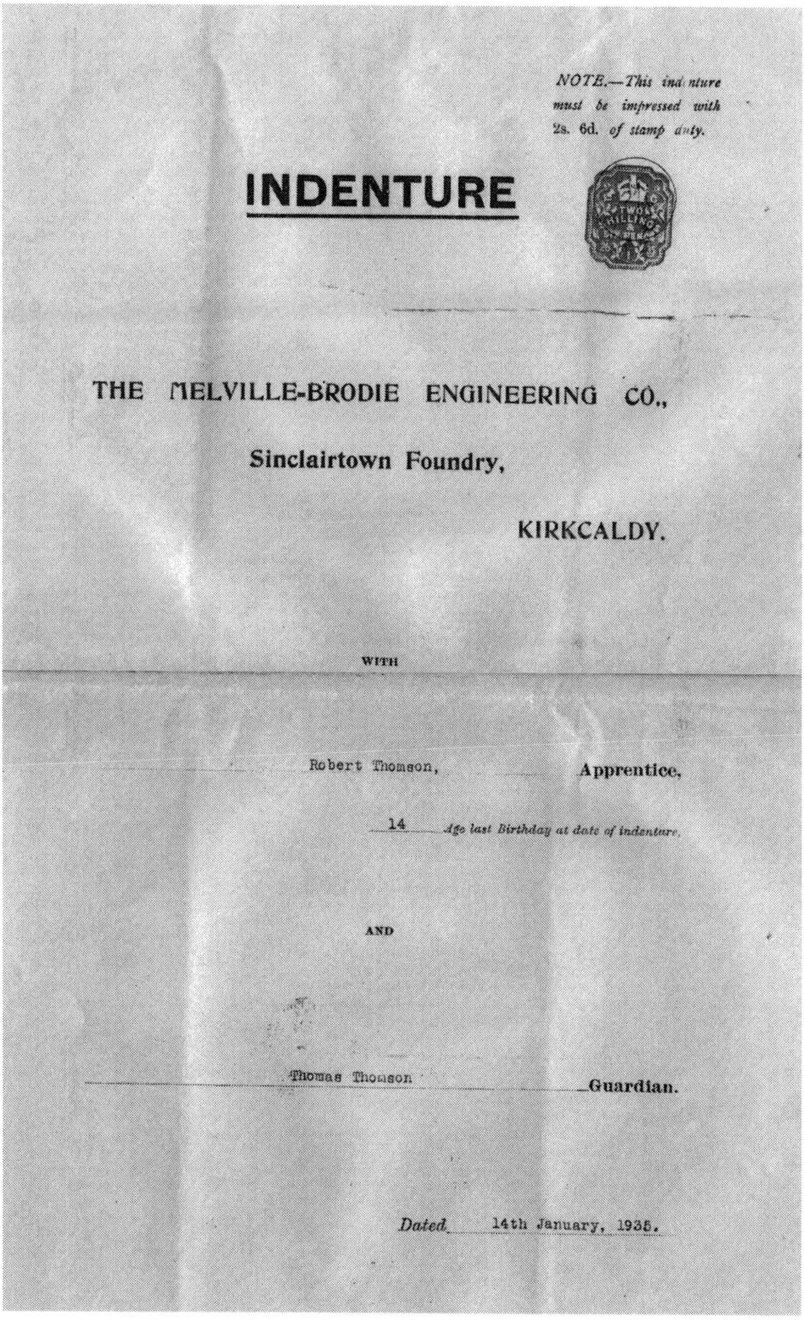

NOTE.—This indenture must be impressed with 2s. 6d. of stamp duty.

INDENTURE

THE MELVILLE-BRODIE ENGINEERING CO.,

Sinclairtown Foundry,

KIRKCALDY.

WITH

Robert Thomson, **Apprentice,**

14 *Age last Birthday at date of indenture.*

AND

Thomas Thomson **Guardian.**

Dated 14th January, 1935.

(hereinafter called "The Employers"), of the first part, and

(hereinafter called "The Apprentice"), residing at 84, Harriet Street, KIRKCALDY.

of the second part, with consent of Thomas Thomson

(hereinafter called "The Guardian"), of the third part, as his curator and administrator in law, in manner herein stated, THAT IS TO SAY :—

2. BINDING: The Apprentice of his own free will, with consent of the Guardian, hereby puts and binds himself as a Trade Apprentice with and to the Employers in the Turning Department of their business subject to the provisions herein for the full and complete space of five years. The Apprentice and the Guardian bind themselves jointly and severally, that during the continuance of this indenture the Apprentice shall industriously and faithfully serve the Employers and promptly obey all the lawful rules, regulations, and commands of the Employers, and of their officers, representatives and authorised employees, and shall conceal and in no ways reveal the secrets of the Employers' business or of the business of their customers, and also that the Apprentice will not do or commit, or suffer to be done or committed, any waste, damage or other injury to the property or goods of the Employers, and will not lend such property or goods to any person without the consent of the Employers.

3. PROBATIONARY PERIOD: Of the aforementioned period of five years, the first three months is to be regarded as a probationary period in that if the Employers shall find that the Apprentice is not likely to prove suitable for training as a Trade Apprentice, it shall be competent to the Employers to discharge said Apprentice, and contrariwise, if the said Apprentice finds that the trade to which he has put himself is not to be suitable, through ill health or any other satisfactory reason which can be proved, it shall be competent for the Guardian to withdraw said Apprentice from such engagement, failing which the aforementioned period of three months having been served, it shall be understood that this Agreement is binding for the full period of five years.

4. REGULARITY AND ATTENTION: The Apprentice shall be regular and punctual in his attendance, well behaved and attentive to all instructions given him and shall behave himself civilly and respectfully to his Employers and their customers; and the Guardian shall discharge the whole obligations incumbent upon him in virtue of this indenture.

5. EMPLOYERS TO INSTRUCT THE APPRENTICE: FOR WHICH CAUSES AND ON THE OTHER PART the Employers agree to take the said Robert Thomson as their Apprentice during the said period in the Turning Department of their business on the conditions of this indenture; moreover, the Employers bind themselves to instruct, or cause to be instructed, in so far as they reasonably can do so, the said Apprentice in the handicraft of the said Department and the requisite knowledge of the trade appertaining thereto, and the Apprentice shall use all the diligence and ability of which he is capable to become proficient therein.

6. HOURS PER YEAR: It is declared that each year of the apprenticeship shall consist of 2350 hours, or the statutory number of hours which may hereafter be laid down by law, and that no year shall be held to be completed until that number of hours in the year in question has been served by the Apprentice.

7. OVERTIME: The Apprentice shall, when necessary, at the request of the Employers, and subject to the Factory Acts and any other Act for the time applicable to the Employers' business, work overtime. Declaring, however, that each hour of overtime worked by the Apprentice shall count as one hour and one-half, and each hour worked by the Apprentice on Sundays shall be reckoned as two hours.

8. OUTSIDE WORK: The Employers may require the Apprentice to work on the premises or at any place within Great Britain or Ireland where they happen to be employed.

9. LEAVE-OFF HOLIDAYS: The Apprentice shall not absent himself from the Works except on leave first asked and obtained from the Foreman in charge of his Department, but the Apprentice shall be allowed all usual Public or Trades Holidays observed in the Works before counting lost time falling to be made up.

10. In case the Apprentice shall be absent owing to illness, a Doctor's or Guardian's letter, satisfactory to the Employers, must be sent to the Works, failing which absence shall be considered absence without leave, unless an explanation satisfactory to the Employers is given. In case of allowance for illness, not more than six weeks in any one year to be allowed as time counted for Apprenticeship. This also applies to accidents outwith Employer's control. In case of accidents in Employer's Works and for which compensation is paid, not more than eight weeks in any one year will be counted as time served, except under special arrangement.

11. No payment shall be due during any period the Apprentice is absent through sickness or on holiday or from any other cause, nor for any time lost on account of the closure of the Works for any cause.

12. PENALTY FOR ABSENCE: And should the Apprentice absent himself for any cause without leave, except through sickness or accident, he shall be liable to pay as liquidated damages the sum of 2s. 6d. for each day, and further, each hour of such absence shall be made up by one and a half hours' extra service.

13. RATES OF PAY: The Employers agree to pay the Apprentice for each week of actual duty preformed and proportionately for less or more in accordance with the terms of this indenture and in compliance with such rules, regulations, and commands as the Employers may from time to time prescribe, the following sums respectively :—

For the First Year	7/6d.	Shillings per week.
For the Second Year	10/-	Shillings per week.
For the Third Year	12/6d.	Shillings per week.
For the Fouth Year	15/-	Shillings per week.
For the Fifth Year	20/-	Shillings per week.
~~For the Sixth Year~~	----------	~~Shillings per week.~~

The terms and conditions of this indenture have been completed to our satisfaction.

FOR THE [illegible] CO.

(Signature) John Brodie *(Employers).*

Date 14th [illegible] 1946

APPENDIX SIX

Melville-Brodie Company: Owners and Engineers

Wm. Melville
R. Henderson
W. Kilgour
R. B. Brodie
J. Brodie
J. Gordon (Bertram)
H. Mann
D. Bertram
J. Bayne [manager]
W. Williamson [manager]

EMPLOYEES IN 1940

(List compiled by Bob Thomson)

FRONT OFFICE
Mr. McKay [manager]
David Grear
James Hepburn
Bob Boyle [jun.]

DRAWING OFFICE
Sandy Allison
Alex Henderson
T. Simpson
Mrs J. Fraser
John Skobie (jun.)

PATTERN SHOP
George Ingles [foreman]
Alex Farr
Joe Walsh

STORE
David Gibb
+ 2 apprentices

BLACKSMITHS
Will Dunsire [foreman]
Pete Douglas
W. Lowther
+ one other blacksmith
S. Bayne [apprentice + 1 other]
Dave [hammerman]

FOUNDRY
Bob Williamson [foreman]
Bob Marin [core maker]
Mr. Colville
Bob Brough
B. Dick
J. Birrell [apprentice]
A. Fenton [dresser]

TURNERS
John Knox
Tom Patterson

TURNERS ...
J. Dewar
R. Speed
T. Crombie
S. Simpson
W. Findlay
W. Whittaker
A. Galloway
S. Johnstone
D. Givens
T. Gordon
B. Stevens
R. Thomson
Mr. Hunter

MACHINE MEN
D. Russell
J. Arthur
J. Gibb
W. Duncan
G. Brown
D. Skinner
G. Sharp
D. Donaldson
J. Smail
A. Brooks
J. Christie
D. Potter
G. Low

CRANE
B. Walker

FITTING SHOP (gallery)
Charlie Ralley [chargehand]
Hugh Pattison
W. chapman [apprentice]

FITTING SHOP
John Oliver [foreman]
D. Taylor

FITTING SHOP...
H, Stag
J. Welsh
J. Irvine
D. Syme
J. Gibson
Mr. Black
A. Kidd
Mr. Nicholson
D. Yardley
W. Stuart
H. Pattison
T. Pattison
R. McDonald [labourer]
P. Cuthill [crane driver]

MARKING OFF
Archie Watt
C. Kerss
Maintenance Fitter
Alf Holland

THE FIFTIES, SIXTIES & SEVENTIES

OFFICE

Mr. McKay (manager)
Miss Winnie Collins (P.A/Sec.)
Wilma Reid (secretarial)
Mary Gilmour (secretarial)
Barbara Orminson
John Whitehill
Jim Dunsire
Jim Heburn
Jim Swan
Alex Kidd

DRAWING OFFICE

Tam Simpson
Dave Griffiths
Tom Simpson
Bill Robertson
Gus McDonald
Gordon Leitch
Bill Henderson
Ian Low
Maureen Griffiths (tracer)

STORES

Ken Crichton
Jim Gibb

PATTERN SHOP

Alex Morgan [Foreman]
John Greig
Jim Samson
Wallace Buist
John Robertson
Alex Smith

PATTERN SHOP ...

Ronnie Keith
George Grant
Alan Auchterlonie
Additional staff after move to East March St., 1963-64
Jimmy Soutar
Alex Bell
Jim Shaw
Bill McLean
Peter Ashworth
+ 2 others

FOUNDRY

Mr. Williamson [Foreman]
Ronnie Fleming
Eck Fenton
Jock Colville
Mr. Naylor
Bob Brough
Alex O' Shea
Sandy Donald
Chick Syme
Dunc Nicol
Davy Haig
Jock Glass
Jimmy Gibb
Will Scott
Jimmy Allison
Abby Downie
Jimmy Marks
Freddie Beck
Shug Ross
Willie Simpson
Bert Lindsay

FOUNDRY ...
Will Alexander
Eck Ritchie
Aund Cunningham
Jim Bates

SMIDDY
W. Dunsire [Foreman]
Dave McArthur
Sandy Millar
Harry Baillie

MACHINE SHOP
Dick Ross [Foreman]
Willie Black
Andrew Farr
Dave Donaldson
Wull Findlay
Tam Crammie
Walter Rymick
Sharma Vedyas
Willie Farquarson
Henry Gilmour
Tam Patterson
Albert Kidd
George Brown
Wull Lindsay
Vic Wenham
Jim Gibb
Sam Murdoch
John McMillan
Matt Morrison
Sandy Pickett
Sandy Pennycuick
Bill Cunningham
Dougie Reid
John Wishart

MACHINE SHOP ...
George Punler
Dave Davidson
Bob Murray
Jim Pratt

ELECTRICIANS
Bill Wallace
Jim Scott

FITTING SHOP
Bill Rose [Foreman]
Wull Mutch
Don Barclay
John Barnes
Jim Honeyman
Gus Robb
Alfie Holland
Alex Bowie
Arch Watt
Drew Sneddon
Chic Beveridge
Bill Simpson
Pete Dall
Jim Doyle
Chic Brews
George Yardley
Dave McAuley
Harry Duncan
Dave Syme
Willie Nicholson
Bill Lonie
Wilber Masterton
Chic Renton
Bob Davie
Dave Crawford
Bob Thomson
Frank McLeod

GALLERY
Charlie Ralley

LORRIES
Willie Lessels
George McCormack

CRANE
Pete Cuthill

LABOURER
Arch McGilvary

PHOTOGRAPHIC ACKNOWLEDGMENTS

Front cover

- Drawing of the Melville-Brodie building by Bill Robertson.
- Five-roll linoleum mixer. Mrs. June Shanks photo collection.
- Replica of the Melville-Brodie logo made by John Creig, photo by G. Mazzei.

Page 7
(1) Planning the project, 21 August 2013; (2) Dougie Reid (L) and John Greig (R) interviewed by Margaret Bennett (3) Willie Black interview. Photos by G. Mazzei.

Page 8
(4) Ronnie Fleming (L) and John Greig (R) discuss drawings
(5) Left to Right: Margaret, Dougie, John, Ronnie and Willie, 2013 (6) Collecting drawings, plans and photos, 19 February 2014. Photos by G. Mazzei.

Page 9
(7) Dougie explains drawings to Chris Miles, 19 February 2014
(8 & 9) John and Dougie discuss historical information of Melville-Brodie Eng. Co with Margaret, 26 August 2014. Photos by G. Mazzei.

Page 10
Almost ready to go to press: Margaret Bennett with Ronnie Fleming and Dougie Reid. Monday, 1st June 2015. Photo by G. Mazzei.

Page 21
Kirkcaldy map showing of the site of the Dunnikier Colliery (Pannie Pit), the Denfield Power Loom Works on Factory Road. [Ordinance Survey map, 1894].

Page 22
Drawing from a planning application, 1957, which shows the site of Melville-Brodie Engineering Company in relation to the Denfield Power Loom factory and Fife Forge. [Fife Archive Collection]

Page 29
Robert Burt Brodie in the drawing office, c. 1910. Mrs. June Shanks photo collection.

Page 34
Replica of the Melville-Brodie logo made by John Greig, photo by G. Mazzei.

Page 35
Journeymen and apprentices, Dysart, in the early 1880s. Mrs. June Shanks photo collection.

Page 35
Robert Burt Brodie's advanced certificate in Machine Construction and Drawing, 1888. Mrs. June Shanks collection.

Page 36
Junction Road from St. Clair Street, 1908. At the top of the street, in the distance, is Melville-Brodie Engineering Company. [George Proudfoot, Kirkcaldy Civic Society; in *Bygone Kirkcaldy* Eric Eunson, Stenlake Publishing 1991].

Page 36
Portrait of Robert Burt Brodie. Mrs. June Shanks photo collection.

Page 37
Melville-Brodie workforce, c. 1934. Mrs. June Shanks photo collection.

Page 37
Melville-Brodie engineers, makers and fitters of the machinery for Tayside Lino Factory, Newburgh, Fife, 1912. Mrs. June Shanks photo collection.

Page 38

Falkland Lino Factory (derelict in 2014). It was officially opened in 1934. Photo by G. Mazzei.

Page 38 and 39
Programme of Proceedings during the opening of the new Scottish Co-op linoleum factory for Flakland, Fife, on Saturday, 23rd June 1934. Mrs. June Shanks collection.

Page 40
Celebration for the coronation of King George V, Kirkcaldy, 11 May, 1911. Mrs. June Shanks photo collection.

Page 40
Councillor Robert Burt Brodie's invitation to a Civic Reception in Kirkcaldy for Field Marshall Earl Haig, 1920. Mrs. June Shanks Collection.

Page 41
Staff outing, Robert B. Brodie in the centre, 1909. Mrs. June Shanks photo collection.

Page 41
Melville-Brodie foremen's outing in front of the Lomond Hotel, Kinnesswood. Pipe smoking genttleman, John Bayne. Robert Burt Brodie extreme right, c. 1913. Photo from Tom Harris.

Page 42
John (Jock) Brodie, Royal Flying Corps, c. 1914; Robert Burt Brodie in the garden of Milfield House, late 1920s; Robert Burt Brodie, standing by his Buick, c. 1929 and John (Jock) Brodie, same pose, different Buick, 1930s. Mrs. June Shanks photo collection.

Page 43
Milfield House, Falkland, Robert B. Brodie's family home from the late 1920s and Melville-Brodie outing 1920s. Mrs. June Shanks photo collection.

Page 58
Drawing of the Melville-Brodie building by Bill Robertson.

Page 66
Maureen Griffiths and her drawing instruments. Photos by Margaret Bennett

Page 86
Bill Robertson standing beside a new part for paper making-machinery, inside the end bay of the fitting shop. Melville-Brodie Engineering Co, c. 1968.

Page 87
Apprentices beside a horizontal lathe, 1959. Back row: Sandy Pennycuick, Sandy Picket, Dougie Reid. Front row: Eddie Murdoch (Sammy), Ronnie Fleming, Bill Simpson, John (Jock) MacMillan. Matthew Morrison photo collection.

Page 88
The boys in boilersuits, apprentices. From left: Bill Cunningham (Tipper), Dougie Reid, Mathew Morrison (Matt) and Eddie Murdoch (Sammy), c.1958. Matthew Morrison photo collection.

Page 88
Apprentices, back row: Sandy Pennycuik, Ronnie Fleming, John McMillan (Jock), Sandy Picket and Eddie Murdoch. Front: Bill Simpson & Dougie Reid. Matthew Morrison photo collection.

Page 89
Journeymen craftsmen. Inscription on the back is: 'Senior brotherhood just prior to the one trouser leg being raised, 1959.' Front left: Sharma, Tom Cramey, Willie Black, Tom Patterson and Andrew Farr. Matthew Morrison photo collection.

Page 90
Mary Gilliard sitting at Maureen Griffiths' desk in the Drawing Office, mid-1950's.

Page 91
Apprentices getting together. From Left: Dougie Reid, Bill Simpson, Eddie Murdoch (Sammy), Eck Murray and Sandy Pennycuick, 1960. Matthew Morrison photo collection.

Page 91
Staff of the Drawing Office 1950's: Gordon Leitch (back), Gus MacDonald (L), Maureen Griffiths in her floral overall, and Bill Robertson (R).

Page 95
Nothing serious, but you'll no dae it again!
Losing a finger-tip or the end of a thumb turns skilled craftsman (Willie and Ronnie) into convincing teachers of Health and Safety. Photo by G. Mazzei

Page 99
Chisel, Melville-Brodie collection. Photo by G. Mazzei.

Page 103
Ronnie's tools. Photo by G. Mazzei.

Page 104
Ronnie in his 'wee foondry' and some of his tools. Photo by M. Bennett.

Page 105
The troon and the wee troon, stamped with the Monk and the deuk's neb, hand made of brass, the date stamped 1884. Photo by M. Bennett

Page 106
The pattern made by John Greig and the cast by Ronnie Fleming. Kirkcaldy, 2014. Photo by M. Bennett.

Page 107
Machines: Grace's Guide to British Industrial History includes machines designed and built by Melville-Brodie Engineering Company, <www.gracesguide.co.uk>, from top: Six-roll Mill Melville-Brodie; Three-roll linoleum mixer. Melville-Brodie and Linoleum Printing Machine for 18 Inch. blocks. Melville-Brodie. Grace's Guide industrial collection.

Page 108
Five-Roll linoleum mixers. Mrs. June Shanks photo collection.

Page 109
Melville-Brodie industrial pump,1920, and Linoleum mixer. Mrs. June Shanks photo collection.

Page 110
An industrial pumps designed and made to order by Melville-Brodie. Mrs. June Shanks photo collection.

Page 111
Melville-Brodie cement mixer. Mrs. June Shanks photo collection.

Page 117
The Melville-Brodie float constructed around Mr. Brodies's Buick. The team are all set to go, and so is their driver, Robert Burt Brodie. Mrs. June Shanks photo collection.

Page 118
The works outing – Top photo: left to right: Left to right: Bill Simpson, Arch McGilvray, Dougie Reid, John Whiltehill, Don Barclay, Dave Nicol, Will Brown, Ernie Sharp, Derek White, Charles Brewster, 1960. Matthew Morrison photo collection.

Page 118
Photo bottom left: From left: Arch McGilvary, John Whitehill, Don Barcley, Dave Nicol, Will Brown, Ernie Sharp, Derek White, Charles Brewster and Dougie Reid, 1960. Morrison photo collection.
Page 118
Photo bottom right: Left to right: Matthew Morrison, Dougie Reid and Bill Simpson.1960. Morrison photo collection.

Page 119
There were occasional staff events and always time for a pint on the way home. Front left: Dougie Reid, Chick McCann, Charles Brewster and Dick Shan. Matthew Morrison photo collection.

Page 119
Calling all radio hams! Melville-Brodie engineers on Kirkcaldy Pageant Day (1930s), Mr. Brodie even drive his car! Mrs. June Shanks photo collection.

Page 131
Jacket of the The 7-inch EP (45 rpm) made by Amalgamated Union of Engineering Workers (AUEW): 'We are the Engineers and I'm gonna be an Engineer' sung by Peggy Seeger and Ewan MacColl. Photo by M. Bennett.

Page 132
Letterhead of The Melville-Brodie Engineering Co. Ltd. Kircaldy, 21st September 1962. See the Bertram Logo.

Page 134
Machine drawing of a Haulage Guvernor 1930s, possibly for a patent application.

Page 152 to 161
W. Lindsay's photos of Melville-Brodie years.

Page 162
Unveiling the memorial plaque on the Melville-Brodie site, Kirkcaldy, 14 May, 2014. Photo from top, front left: Willie Black, Margaret Bennett, Councillor Kay Carrington, June Shanks, Dougie Reid, Bob Thomson, representatives of the Fife Council. Second photo June and Bob unveiling the plaque. Third left: Dougie Reid, Ronnie Fleming and John Grieg. Third right: Margaret Bennett and Willie Black. Fourth left: Claire Morrison, Matthew Morisson and Margaret Bennett. Fourth right: Bob Thomson interviewed by Margaret Bennett. Photos by G. Mazzei.

REFERENCES

Books

Buchanan, John F. (1903). *Foundry Nomenclature: the Moulder's Pocket* Dictionary. London & New York: Spon & Chamberlain.

Charles Dickens. (1853). *Household Words: A Weekly Journal.* London: Bradbury & Evans.

Eunson, Eric. (1991). *Bygone Kirkcaldy.* Glasgow: Stenlake Publishing.

Harrison, John G. (2013). *Notes on the History of the Nail Trade in Scotland 1500–1800*, available online via his website, <www.johnscothist.com>).

Hobbs, Sandy, Jim McKechnie, and Michael Lavalette. (1999). *Child Labour: A World History Companion.* Oxford : ABC-Clio.

Palmer, Roy. (1988). *The Sound of History: Songs and Social Comment.* Oxford: Oxford University Press. (Reprinted 1996.

Potter, David. (2013). *'Tis a Hundred Years Syne: Kirkcaldy in World War I.* Kirkcaldy: Kirkcaldy Civic Trust.

Rankin, Frank. (1988). *Guide To Wemyss Caves.* Methil, Fife: Published by Save Wemyss Ancient Caves Society. (Revised and reprinted 2009).

Seeger, Peggy (Ed). (2009). *The Essential Ewan MacColl Songbook: Sixty Years of Songmaking*. Northfield, MN: Loomis-House-Press.

Seeger, Peggy. (1997). *The Peggy Seeger Songbook: Warts and All: Forty Years of Songmaking*. New York: Oak Publications.

Smith, Adam. (1776). *Inquiry into the Nature and Causes of Wealth of Nations*. London: W. Strahan and T. Cadell. (many editions).

Statistical Account of Scotland (Old, OS) 1791–1799, Vol. 18, p. 1 ff.

Statistical Account of Scotland (New, NS) 1834-45, Vol. 9, p. 740 ff.

Tuckett, Angela. (1974). *The Blacksmiths' History: What Smithy*

Workers Gave Trade Unionism. London: Lawrence and Wishart.

Newspapers and Magazines

The Dundee Courier, Oct. 26, 1937 (and various editions).
The Courier, (Fife, various editions).
The Edinburgh Gazette, June 1908 and October 1918 (and various editions).
Labour Monthly, Oct. 1960.
The Glasgow Herald, May 1960.
The Fife Free Press (various editions).

GRACE NOTES SCOTLAND

Grace Notes Scotland is dedicated to identifying and handing on traditions to new generations. All of our projects document (whether in written or oral form), conserve, nurture and promote Scotland's languages and dialects, traditions and skills, oral history, songs, tunes and stories. We work to broaden awareness of, and share our love of, Scotland's 'intangible heritage' (UNESCO 2003) and invite people of all ages, abilities and backgrounds to participate in projects. In giving voice to every generation, we recognise and value the elderly, and encourage the young to appreciate their heritage. Projects enable both current and new generations to benefit from the skills and values of the past so that they may enrich their own lives and communities.

Based near Comrie, Perthshire, the Scottish Charity 'Grace Notes Scotland' (SC040434) was established in 2009. There are three members of the board of directors:

Secretary Liz Elkind is a long-time Trade Union and Trades Council activist. For many years she lectured in Community Education in Edinburgh and was a council member and President of the higher education section of EIS. She was a member of the STUC General Council and served as its President. She loves to sing and is a member of several choirs including 'Protest in Harmony'.

Treasurer Dr Renate Gertz is Freedom of Information & Data Protection Officer for East Lothian Council. A Former lecturer in law at the University of Edinburgh, Rena is also a singer and member of a folk band as well as keen a craftswoman.

Artistic Director Margaret Bennett, who grew up in Skye, is a folklorist, singer, broadcaster and author of several books on Scottish traditions. A former lecturer at the University of Edinburgh, she holds an Honorary Research Fellowship at the University of St Andrews, teaches part-time at the Royal Conservatoire of Scotland in Glasgow, and is Honorary Professor of Antiquities and Folklore at the Royal Academy of Scotland. (www.margaretbennett.co.uk)